TO
THE SOURCE OF WEALTH IN YOU™

Written Especially For

Name

Date

PRAISE FOR
AWAKEN
TO
THE SOURCE OF WEALTH IN YOU™

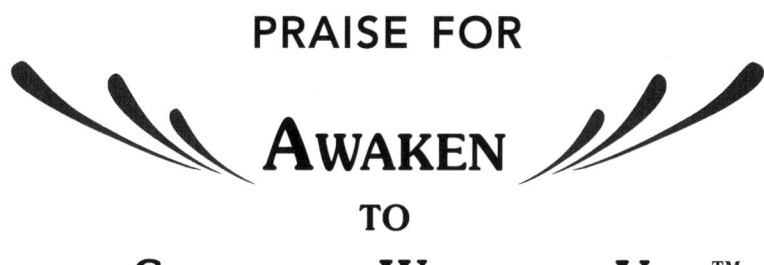

"This wonderful, inspiring book shows you how to achieve real wealth by connecting to your innermost visions, values and beliefs."
—BRIAN TRACY, AMERICA'S LEADING AUTHORITY ON SELF-DEVELOPMENT AND NEW YORK TIMES BESTSELLING AUTHOR

"Think of Awaken to the Source of Wealth in You™ *as your 'Action Guide' to overcoming emotional turbulence. Diana DeMar is brilliant. These principles really will help you live your best life."*
—RANDY PEYSER, AUTHOR OF CRAPPY TO HAPPY & THE POWER OF MIRACLE THINKING

"Diana, your book changed my life. I wouldn't have made a change without it. God bless you forever! You are an angel!"
—RICKI MARTINEZ, MUSICAL DIRECTOR & COMPOSER, PUERTO RICO

"Diana DeMar's Awaken to the Source of Wealth in You™ *principles are simple and will change the way you think, act and live your life in ways you never thought possible. This is a must read book for anyone committed to achieve remarkable results and true lasting success!"*
—JAY SILMAN, OWNER OF JAY SILMAN TAX SERVICES, NEW YORK

AWAKEN
TO
THE SOURCE OF WEALTH IN YOU™

*117 Secrets to Reconnect
to Your Divine Power*

DIANA DEMAR

DIANA DEMAR SUCCESS
SHERMAN OAKS, CALIFORNIA

Awaken to the Source of Wealth in You™
117 Secrets to Reconnect to Your Divine Power
by Diana DeMar

Copyright © 2011 Diana DeMar. All rights reserved.
Published by: **Diana DeMar Success;** P.O. Box 55741; Sherman Oaks, CA 91413-5741 U.S.A.
Orders@DianaDeMarSuccess.com; www.DianaDeMarSuccess.com; www.TheSourceOfWealthInYou.com
Phone: (310) 742-4103

Printed in the United States of America. No part of this book may be reproduced or transmitted in any form or by any means, electronic or mechanical, including photocopying, recording or by any information storage and retrieval system, other than for "fair use" as brief quotations embodied in articles and reviews, without prior written permission of the publisher. This book is sold subject to the condition that it shall not, by way of trade or otherwise, be lent, re-sold, hired out, or otherwise circulated without the publisher's prior consent in any form of binding or cover other than that in which it is published and without a similar condition including the condition being imposed on the subsequent purchaser. This book represents the works of Diana DeMar, the originator of The Source of Wealth in You™; a series of books and applied self-development and meditation-healing technology. It's presented to its readers as a record of the author's observations, experiences, and experiments of the human body, mind, and spirit in its connection with the universal energy, God. It is not a statement of claims made by the author. The benefits and goals of The Source of Wealth in You™ soul technology can be attained only by the dedicated efforts of the reader.

WARNING: This book is structured in a proprietary format specific to The Source of Wealth in You™ books that is: a combination of the author's quotation, followed by author's contemplation, and followed by the reader's written response. Any copying of this specific book structure would be considered an infringement of The Source of Wealth in You™ books' copyright and identity.

DISCLAIMER: The author of this book does not dispense medical advice or prescribe the use of any technique as a form of treatment for physical or medical problems without the advice of a physician, either directly or indirectly. The intent of the author is to offer information to help you in your quest for self-discovery, awakening, transformation and well-being. Never disregard professional medical advice or delay in seeking it! The author and publisher assume no responsibility for the actions of the reader. The contents of this book, including text, graphics, images, and other material contained in this book ("Content") are for informational purposes only. The stories in this book are true; however, the names have been changed to maintain privacy.

†DIANA Diana and Design is a registered trademark owned by Diana DeMar © 2001, © 2008, © 2011

†DIANA
The Source of Wealth in You™ is a registered trademark owned by Diana DeMar © 2009, © 2010, © 2011

Contributing Editors: T. N. R. Rogers; Jo-Anne Craine of Type A Creative; Gail Koffman
Interior Design: Jill Cooper; Sunny B. DiMartino

Library of Congress Cataloging-in-Publication Data
DeMar, Diana.
Awaken to the Source of Wealth in You™: 117 Secrets to Reconnect to Your Divine Power/Diana DeMar

ISBN-13: 978-0-983-03260-1 (paperback)
ISBN-10:   0-983-03260-2

1. Self-Help 2. Success 3. Inspiration

Edition: 1st Edition

Copyright © 2011 Diana DeMar: Balancing Act Principle©, I Release My Past Meditation©, I Release the Abundance That I Am Affirmation©, My Soul's Mission Affirmation©, Principle of Attraction©, Principle of Cause and Effect©, Principle of Giving©, Principle of Letting Go©, Principle of Planting a Seed©, Principle of Restriction©, Principle of Selective Desire©, Principle of the Opposite Action©, Principle of Transferable Energy©, Rhythm of Your Heart Awakening Meditation©, The Source of Wealth in You™ Ego Principle©, The Source of Wealth in You™ Meditation©, The Source of Wealth in You™ Teachings Core Belief©

2010937297

*From my soul, I devote this book to you.
May you Awaken to the Source of Wealth in You™ residing within.
I love you!*

Contents

III	Preface
1	Introduction
21	Get Started
35	Resolve The Past; Remain in the Present
57	Release The Emotional Mind and Ego Traps
69	Create Yourself!
91	Everything Is Energy
109	Change!
121	Discover the Balance
145	You're the Source of Wealth
171	Dare to Be You! Sex Is Love!
195	Our World Is Awakening
219	Summary of the 117 Secrets
227	Glossary
239	Resources
241	About the Author

My INTENTION is to communicate the truth that each one of us is here for a reason.

My MISSION is to help others see beyond the boundaries of the material world, through the illusions of everyday life.

My PURPOSE is to assist you on the path toward balance and authenticity by giving you the tools, so you can rediscover, reconnect to, and rely on
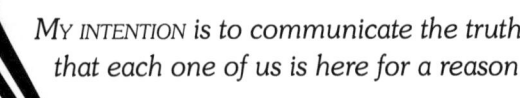

Preface

WITHIN THE LAST FOUR YEARS, I've become very rich. I discovered an endless Source of Wealth and I draw from it on a day to day basis. I want to give you the key to *The Source of Wealth in You*™ so you can become rich too. There is an expression I've heard from successful people: "If I told you the secret to getting rich, it wouldn't be a secret anymore!" This may be true for the temporary Source of Wealth in the material world (money); however, the Source of Wealth I'm talking about is the only real and permanent Source and it contains anything and everything you can think of—not just money but true happiness. Unless you reconnect to the permanent inner Source of Wealth you will not become rich in the outer, material world. Even if you do, it'll be short lived and easily lost.

I spend a large part of my life in silence by myself. I love listening to the sound of silence but when I get out of my house I fully immerse myself in the joy of being with other souls, dancing and celebrating life with them.

Before my awakening, not long ago I was on a constant search. I read Eastern texts and listened to motivational and self help audio programs. Today, though I keep up with what's going on in "the world," I still prefer to sit down and simply, yet consciously *breathe*. I have found reality in a single breath. I continue to discover my "inner world" through ancient, modern and high tech means along with my own experiments and observations. But my sense of reality comes mainly from my Higher Self. The Higher Self is that part of your being that deals with the truth.

The realizations in this book come from the core of my being, from my truth and experiences and with little traditional research. These words flowed from me naturally and the process has been cleansing, purifying, and effortless. The life truths I have written here are simple, easy to understand and to apply to your everyday life—if you only allow them.

If any of the terms I use are unfamiliar to you, see the *Glossary* in the back that I have provided. In fact, you may want to skim through the *Glossary* before you start reading Secret 1 just to familiarize yourself with the information there. Additionally, if you would like to refer to a specific secret, see the *Summary of the 117 Secrets* that provides an at-a-glance listing of the 117 Secrets for your convenience.

The writings in this book are for everyone. Each step of wisdom written here will have a unique meaning to each individual. Write down what it means to you and how you're going to apply it in your life. *This is what starting to express your own individuality looks like.* Answer the questions and follow through on what you have written and you'll see a change. If you cannot relate to some of the content simply move on. Do not allow yourself to get stuck trying to figure it out. *This is all part of learning to let go.* Success and happiness come with their own tools and skills and with your ability to apply them in the material world.

I feel strongly that these writings will resonate within and even be life-changing for most of you. I can't wait for your transformation to begin and am looking forward to hearing all about it!

Diana DeMar
January, 2011
Los Angeles, California

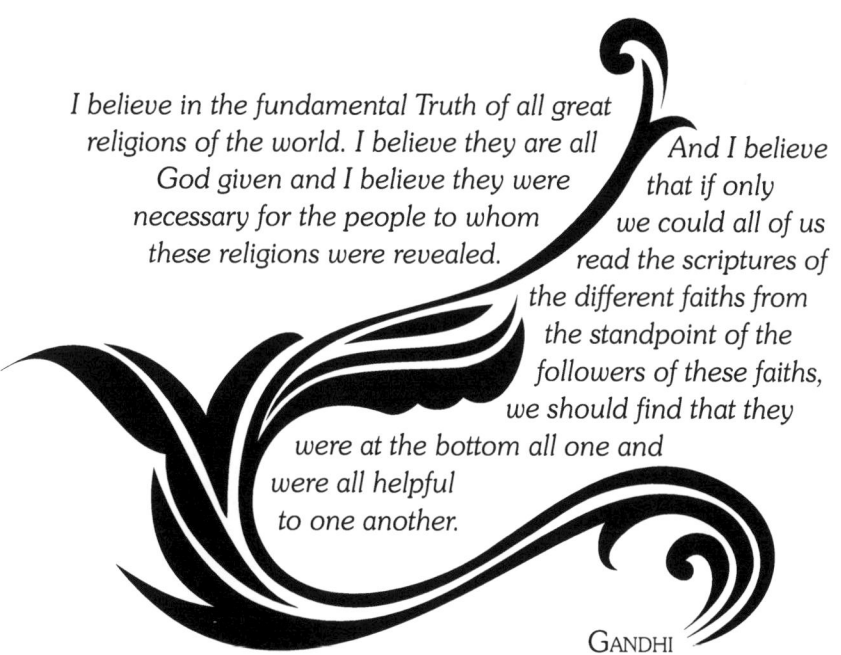

I believe in the fundamental Truth of all great religions of the world. I believe they are all God given and I believe they were necessary for the people to whom these religions were revealed. And I believe that if only we could all of us read the scriptures of the different faiths from the standpoint of the followers of these faiths, we should find that they were at the bottom all one and were all helpful to one another.

Gandhi

*There's nothing to worry about,
relax...and detach from it...let go.
Like an ocean wave,
life's naturally gliding where it's supposed to.
Surrender to the peaceful transformation,
release the desires and doubts.
You're settling in, constantly changing,
immersing into the flow.*

Introduction

When I was little, I wanted to be an astronaut and fly in space. One of my first childhood memories is of taking an umbrella from the hall closet and sneaking out onto the roof of our house. My idea was to use the umbrella as a parachute. I recall the feeling of excitement fluttering in my stomach as I stood on the edge of the roof. Then I jumped down into the soil garden, and well, I don't remember the rest. Obviously, I didn't fly down gently but had a rather rough crash landing; however, it didn't dampen my spirits. I was pleased with myself for trying.

My family didn't pay much attention to my childhood dreams. Knowing how my mom, dad, and all my relatives think—based strictly on society's rules and what the neighbors would say or think about them—I'm sure they thought flying in space was for boys. Their only desire for me was to attain a prestigious title and to have a secure life. I graduated as a physician assistant to please my parents. There's another book I could write about my childhood. For now, I'll just choose to stay positive, in the now, in the present moment.

During my early teenage years I kept running away from home with my cousin who is five years older than I am but we never got very far. I was a wild child, and together, my cousin and I hatched crazy plans. She financed our travels and planned our escapes and in exchange I would do whatever she wanted. I was always doing things to please others, whether it was my parents, my cousins or my friends. My frustration and sadness stemmed from not having the confidence to know that true happiness came from within.

Most of my life, until several years ago, I felt like dying most of the time. I went through a lot of pain and suffering because I had no idea who I was and what I was supposed to do with my life. I had a "life," but I didn't know what to do with it. I was waiting for this life to pass so I could get closer to the end, to my death. That wasn't easy either; the waiting. I spent five years trying to figure out how to die but I failed at it. In the meantime, during an endless search, I discovered meditation. This, for me, was "the answer," the secret to my being alive today. It always will be.

Before my awakening, I was going through life day after day, plodding along like a caterpillar, not even dreaming that I could ever take flight—until I was shaken, for which I'm grateful.

For more than five years, from 2000 to 2005, I spent most of my life in bed—lost, detached, in emotional pain, suffering, full of depression, turmoil, anger, and hatred, self destructive, without hope or direction in my life. The daily contact I had with the outside world was through the telephone. The people who seemed to care about me spent hours on the phone to help me get out of bed. Nothing they did worked. I barely managed to complete two music CD projects. I was depressed, even debilitated in many ways. I was just passing time, wanting to die but afraid to do anything about it, waiting for my life to run its course. However, I didn't stop searching. I knew that someday there would be a light at the end of the tunnel.

On December 19, 2005, I saw the first sign of hope in meditation when I felt the transcendence of my body. I then knew there was more to life.

I spent the next three years in meditation. Following a number of anxiety and panic attacks, for which I was treated, I went through an experience on August 7, 2007, that I still find incredible and almost impossible to describe or understand. When I lay down to sleep that night, I suddenly found myself gasping for air, unable to breathe or get up to make a phone call. It got very, very cold, freezing, like nothing I had ever felt or known before, and I felt my body shaking uncontrollably, yet still lying perfectly horizontal, but inflexible, straight, and tight. The shaking became rough. I saw my body lifting up about 20 inches from my bed. I was watching my body freeze. I looked at my skin color too, which was different—white, pale, as if the blood had been drained out.

The rest is history. Everything changed for me. Today, I still ask myself if I am now dead or alive. I really do not wish you to experience anything like this transition from living to something else—I'm still unsure what to call it and what it was. Whatever it was, it marked the end of my being lost and of my unbearable suffering.

My dream of flying in space came true—through meditation. When I meditate I feel the transcendence of my body like a weightless feather moving up into the infinite. Here I am: ready, willing, and able to live again and so much more than that! I have truly awakened to who I am and to the reason I'm here today.

Today, I look back and am amazed at the "new Diana" I am now. The Diana back then seems to me like someone I've met whose face is familiar but I don't really recognize: a phantom version of myself, but not me. I cannot even comprehend the person I was just four years ago.

I really wanted to die back then because I couldn't bear it all. I had burdened myself with so much sorrow and guilt from the past that it just became too much for me. It was very heavy to carry around so I was literally bed bound for a few years! When I came close to death, or died, I obviously released the pain and suffering. Finally I shed the baggage I was carrying! I became aware of the energy that I am. I was stuck in my physical body back then but now I am more than a body—I am energy. I still have my body but I'm a soul, a spirit—pure and not damaged anymore. Today, I operate from a different place—from my Higher Self—from Truth.

Awakening and transformation are possible and can be simple too. I am here to show you an easier way so you don't have to go through more than is necessary unless you enjoy pain, drama and playing a victim of life's circumstances. If you do, you won't impress anyone or get more attention, I guarantee you. I tried to get all the love from the world but I found myself depressed because I couldn't get the attention I craved. Life's too short for that. You want some real thrills and excitement, right?

I know many of you are in the same place where I was a few years ago: lost, depressed, confused and unhappy. I do not want you to go through the same experiences. Through this book I promise to awaken you and help you get rid of the baggage you carry that is so heavy it suffocates you. I am here to assist you to transform and to enlighten. I have a secret to reveal: *The Source of Wealth in You*™ —the never-ending Source of Wealth. It's the only real and permanent Source of Wealth there is. I'm going to help you to reconnect to your authentic self, your spirit and God. This is the only way to success and happiness. Nothing else matters. Miracles are waiting to be manifested through you. I know that for sure. Come with me and I'll show you how.

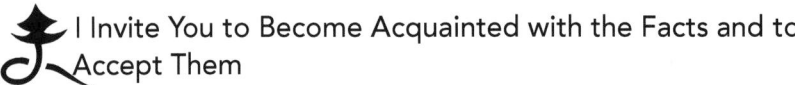 I Invite You to Become Acquainted with the Facts and to Accept Them

The biggest reward for a thing well done is to have done it.

VOLTAIRE

You are the most important person in your life. Your life depends on your self knowledge. People are always looking for information from Sources outside of themselves. Why are you more interested in others than yourself? You can spend your whole life frustrated and unhappy because of doubts, fear, and the unwillingness to discover who you really are. But when you do discover who you are, your life's mission and purpose will be naturally revealed to you. Your life will become meaningful, full of joy and happiness.

Each one of us is unique. There isn't another person out there like you. There might be similarities, but an exact match does not exist. Your inner, natural tendencies you came to this world with, combined with the outer influences of society, make up your personality.

There are always two sides to everything: the alpha and the omega; the Sun and the Moon; the yin and the yang; the "polar opposites" of north and south. Begin today to always consider the two sides. You are created a certain way. Most of us believe we are created by God. But it is your responsibility to continue to create the life given to you by God. We're blessed with an incredible opportunity to create our life on Earth. I strongly support that this is why God created us. God gave you a beginning but the continuation is up to you. Reading alone does not please God but taking action is the answer to living in harmony with God. The life given to you is a life of free will. You can choose to live it however you want. I know this book will help you to begin to make great choices on how to live your life.

The truth is that most people spend their whole life sleepwalking. The PRINCIPLE OF CAUSE AND EFFECT© (aka Karma) is a constant. When you ignore what you came here to do in this lifetime it's possible that you will come back to start all over again. How long do you want to keep doing so? What is standing in your way to truly live a meaningful life, to discover your life's purpose and mission so you can rise to a different level of existence and end the cycle of birth and death and of pain and suffering?

We came here to correct ourselves: to change, to improve and to grow. One of the greatest reasons you are having difficulty getting to know yourself is unawareness. Why do you keep making the same mistakes over and over again? Why do you choose to remain a victim of life's circumstances? How aware are you of your repetitive, negative thoughts? How selective are you of the thoughts that are to be let into your mind and the others that are to be kept out? Are you "walking your talk" or do you just talk?

Keep asking yourself the questions and always write down the answers. This is how you make history! There are certain questions that can easily reveal who you are on the inside and what you are gifted with and those answers hold the potential to manifest on the outside and re-create a new you—all of which you're not yet aware of. It's exciting!

I challenge you to take action. This book is intended to be a fun manual to help you to awaken. It is structured in a certain way so you can actively participate by writing down your thoughts and keep them organized in one place—here in this book. *This is what taking action looks like.* After you have written and answered the questions, then get going! This book will motivate you to act on what you've read and written. When you feel a bit stuck, randomly open a page and embrace the message it holds for you. My energy is with you, always.

Become practical. Remember that certain emotions will prevent you from taking action. Consider them but keep in mind that they will often keep you stuck, unable to progress and take a step forward. The truth is that change and transformation are natural processes of life so consciously align yourself with it! Doubts, insecurity, and making mistakes are part of the process. Take action, regardless!

The Source of Wealth in You™ is waiting to be *awakened*. If you could only see clearly you'd be amazed. After you've practiced the 117 Secrets you'll be able to transform what looks like the impossible into a possibility. This is what you truly are—a Source of Wealth, potential, love and energy.

Begin today to see and focus on the positive side of yourself, life, people, events and your environment. Keep in mind that anything you're dealing with right now will work out for the best. This is how the perfect universe, God works. Notice the negative but remember there's a great lesson to learn from even the most unpleasant situation. Stay with this thought and aim to transform your natural negative tendencies into positive ones. It'll strengthen the positive side of your nature. This is exactly how you're going to become light yourself and create it in the lives of others when life presents you with a difficult challenge. Every time I use the word light, I mean love, fun, joy and happiness. I know there isn't anything else that you would like more of!

You need two opposite poles to create light. You can create light by counteracting a negative experience, encounter, etc. (the negative pole) with the opposite—a positive action, reaction and attitude (the positive pole).

When you read this book often you'll find personal issues that need your attention. By writing down your own interpretations and visions and by answering the questions, clarity and solutions will start to pop up. Remember to always keep it simple. Most answers are found in simplicity. Also, be very specific. At the end of each contemplation there is space provided for you to write one paragraph, not a whole page. You want to get right to the point, in this moment, right here, right now, because it's all we have—this very moment.

Relationships are instrumental in our lives. Create and develop a relationship with a spiritual teacher, a life coach or a truly enlightened master. It's very easy to derail—to fall back to old, unwanted habits and routines. Creating an ongoing relationship with someone you can meet with to exchange ideas is very important. A qualified Certified Life Coach can help you redesign your life, keep you on track and focused, motivate and assist you in creating a plan of action and hold you accountable for following through on it. We all have the same struggles within. Whatever you're going through, you are not alone. Others are in the same boat.

The quotations and ideas in this book are universal. They incorporate a little bit of all religions and teachings. When I began the search for myself four years ago I read some Eastern and religious writings. However, I constantly observe, test, and experiment with my knowledge, ideas, and techniques. During meditation, I receive knowledge from my direct contact with the Universal intelligence, God. God is energy. We are made of energy and surrounded by it.

You have it within, anything you can think of, regardless of your background, race, religion, gender, age, or education. My purpose is to awaken you to what you already are: an endless Source of Wealth. Once you accept this fact, your riches from within will automatically begin to manifest out in the material world.

Timing Is Everything

Continuous effort—not strength or intelligence—is the key to unlocking our potential.

WINSTON CHURCHILL

Have you ever noticed that when you expect a prompt answer to your questions or immediate results you become angry and frustrated? And do you realize that on a deeper level, life goes on regardless, and eventually it all works out for the best? This is why continuous, steady effort in your personal knowledge matters.

For example, when you come across something written in this book that bothers you, feels uneasy, or that you don't understand, read it again and then simply move on. Eventually, when you're ready to hear the same message again you'll naturally come back to it. In the meantime, changes within you have occurred.

Human nature is good, yet stubborn and complicated. On the journey of life by being stubborn you create obstacles and barriers that keep you stuck. This gives you a great excuse to play the role of a victim of life circumstances. Is that what you really want? Or is it your mind playing tricks on you?

We are complicated creatures; indeed, with both a positive and a negative side. But that's fine; that's the way it is—you are who you are. Fantasizing about who and what you "should" be will eventually manifest itself in mental illness. Constant awareness, mind control, using the tools and techniques described in this book and writing your thoughts down will get you started on a life journey of discovery, transformation and happiness. Become easy on yourself; love and care for yourself. Remember, there is no destination—only a journey, the voyage of life. Obsessions will only drain you emotionally, physically, mentally and energetically.

This book is designed as your Life Journal. It's precious. Keep it either to yourself or choose who you want to share it with. If you find that you need more space to write than is provided in this book, remember, when being specific, one paragraph is enough space. Practice restriction—humans tend to overdo and to think excessively. Anything in excess complicates life. Life is already complicated.

You're wise, strong, and able to persevere. Anything of value and worth does not come on a silver platter. Either discover it or create it. Remember, "Rome wasn't built in a day." Whatever it takes, you're worth it! You have the answers.

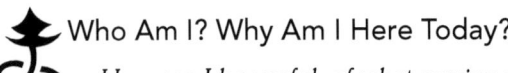Who Am I? Why Am I Here Today?
How can I be useful, of what service can I be? There is something inside me, what can it be?

Vincent van Gogh

Is there anyone who hasn't pondered these questions? I'm certain there isn't. But why do you keep asking yourself? Why do you want the answers?

It's because deep within you know the real truth. You feel that there's more to life than what you can see with your eyes. You know there is God and you want to connect with God. You also want to reveal your true self to yourself and to the world. This is what it takes to achieve authentic success and happiness in life. Wanting to know your natural inclination is to keep searching for it—not simply to keep going through your daily existence like a robot doing the same thing over and over again: eating, sleeping, drinking, working, having sex, watching TV, and so on. How can you be anything if you don't know who you are? It's impossible.

How clearly, honestly and objectively can you see yourself? What are your negative tendencies and how aware are you of them? How deeply do the doubts and fears you live with affect you? If you don't like the answer what can you do to change it?

Look how courageous you are already to take a deeper look at yourself; to see what you don't like, to want to transform and to make it work for you! It's easy to focus on the negative habits and behavior of others but it's hard to notice our own.

We came here, on Earth, to discover who we are in order to make ourselves and others happy. If you do not know who you are you live in ignorance. This is why most people are unhappy and why some remain unhappy all their lives. Life itself is an opportunity. You are making the most of your life's opportunities now by taking these crucial steps to *Awaken to the Source of Wealth in You*™! The answers will come when you least expect them.

So how open are you to start the journey of discovery, keeping in mind that it is a voyage and you'll keep finding new things about yourself and others until you die and maybe beyond? When you look at life this way, you'll always be involved in new discoveries. That is fun and exciting. Engage yourself in these possibilities and you will discover your life's true meaning.

You're an Individual and Life Is Fun

There is nothing either good or bad, but thinking makes it so.

SHAKESPEARE (THE TRAGEDY OF HAMLET)

It's certainly okay to disagree with what I say. You're an individual and your happiness depends on you—on how you see it, on your own interpretation. There's no such thing as right or wrong. It only depends on how you perceive it or choose it to be.

But surely we can all agree on one thing: that having fun in life is everything! Reading and writing in this book is fun! It's meant to be fun, so take advantage of it! When you take life too seriously life will become difficult. It's up to you. Keep in mind that when you take care of yourself the rest will fall into place. As human beings we are born with the power to change our mindsets; we can transform our lives by changing the way we look at things. It's all about perspective. For example, there's really no such thing as "bad weather." Sure, if it's pouring down rain on your outdoor wedding, that's "bad weather," at least to you. When you're the gardener down the street who's been waiting for the drought to end, that's "good weather" to him.

We came on Earth to reclaim our true identity and to express our individuality so we can evolve to a different level of existence. Control of your mind will get you through when things appear difficult or impossible. Each time you catch yourself acting on your negative tendencies, stop it! Learn to control your mind!

The Real You Is Happiness, Perfection, and Love

Take away love and our earth is a tomb.

ROBERT BROWNING

There are two worlds in which we reside—material and spiritual. We spend our daily life in the material world. But it's a temporary world, and it's guaranteed to end for us sooner or later. In order to discover true happiness and to remain in it become consciously aware of and connect to the spiritual world. This world does not have an end. It's a rich world—it holds the wealth of happiness you're searching for. This unseen world is real. It's pure energy, as opposed to the physical world, which is matter with a mixture of energy thrown in. Energy is everything, everywhere, inside and outside of you. You are energy.

The nonphysical, nonmaterial spiritual world is where anything is possible. It's the kingdom where you truly are you. You can rule it in any way you want because it represents the real you—the spirit. The trick in life is to reconnect your body, mind and soul, and to rediscover the balance between these two worlds—the material and the spiritual world.

Happiness is a state, a condition not visible to the eyes. And, yes, you can see when someone is happy, but this is not what I'm talking about here. Happiness originates in the spiritual world. We want to reconnect with the spirit; to our true identity. This is where *The Source of Wealth in You*™ resides. This is God and where God dwells. Most call it God, some Jesus, others Krishna, many Allah. All different names, so many names but for the same thing!

Names are useful in the material world. This is where we seem separate from each other. Yet only in the material, physical world, we are "different" from each other. In the spiritual realm, in God, we are the same, connected, in unity. God is love. God is perfect. God resides within, so you're love and you're perfect too.

You Have a Major Purpose to Fulfill in this Lifetime

As long as you are not aware of the continual law of Die and Be Again, you are merely a vague guest on a dark Earth.

JOHANN WOLFGANG VON GOETHE

A certain period of time on Earth is given to us to learn, to transform, to love and to grow. This is our mission here, on Earth—to complete what we came here to do. Why else would we go through so much turmoil? When it is not completed in this lifetime I believe more turmoil is in store for us. When we grow, we are equipped to transcend to a different level and dimension.

You came into this world in this particular body, shape, form, and makeup with something exceptional to give. Once you master your self you can master anything. Only then you can express yourself in the material world through your own energy. Just energy, I mean it. It's magical. The kind of energy I'm talking about is not only physical but spiritual. Your inner energy reflects your outer physical energy—from the inside out.

Your true self, your spirit, has the ability to create miracles you never thought possible. When you reconnect with the real you—your soul—you work in unison with God, and you create beauty. God is beauty. Remember the saying, "Beauty is in the eye of the beholder?" The beauty I'm talking about has no rules—it's everywhere and it's forever.

There isn't a philosophy or a teacher or a guru that can do it for you. I, Diana DeMar, certainly cannot do it for you. However, I'm here to get you started; to help you set up a solid foundation; to give you the tools, the skills to attain and practice each day; to assist you, guide you, and love you so you can continue the journey on your own.

I want to give you this reminder: you came here to do the work for yourself—to work your own magic and create your own miracles. I know you will, sooner or later. What's needed on your end is what you already have: a longing to reconnect your body and mind with your soul and to tune in your energy to the universal energy, to reconnect with God. This is the ultimate connection—to *The Source of Wealth in You*™. I have revealed the secrets on how to do so. You are about to find out.

Here's What Happened

I did not begin when I was born, nor when I was conceived. I have been growing, developing, through incalculable myriads of millenniums. All my previous selves have their voices, echoes, and promptings in me. Oh, incalculable times again shall I be born.

JACK LONDON

As soon as we are born into the material world our true identity is lost. We take on a bodily form and we are in the hands of other humans. Humans are full of desires, manipulated by their egos and have destructive tendencies.

The human desire destroys everything because the world we come from is abundant and everlasting—from God.

We came to the material world and we lost our sight; we became blind. Everything we learned from our parents or in school was supposed to get us through life somehow but deep inside we're unhappy because we do not own that knowledge; it is not our own discovery, it was given to us. Discovering things for ourselves is at the heart of what it is to be human. This is why, for example, some of our relationships don't last long—because all the curiosity and wonderment that filled us when we first met slowly disappeared. We let it go. We let life go. *When we stop playing life starts playing us.*

The courage to rediscover oneself is what really matters. But so many people are scared of the truth and afraid of finding the truth inside of them so they don't ever try. Are you ready to begin the journey of self discovery? You've already begun!

Here is where a conflict is created—in the two worlds that exist and of which we are an essential part—the physical world and the spiritual world.

- THE PHYSICAL WORLD (AKA THE MATERIAL WORLD). The physical world is the world you can see with your eyes, the world of your senses. You think you want what you see but that isn't it. It's an illusion. This is why you continue to want more because you're confused. You cannot see the truth but you can feel it. The material world is where the mind, the ego dominates you and constantly plays tricks on your pure innocent spirit, but only if you let it. This is its nature. The physical world is guaranteed to end for us sooner or later when we die.
- THE SPIRITUAL WORLD. The spiritual world is pure energy, abundant, and everlasting. It's your soul, spirit and God residing in harmony within.

It's essential to keep in mind that who we may appear on the outside is not who we are at the core of our authentic being. What we seem to be today—our physical, mental, and emotional self—is based on our conditioning by family and society. This conditioning began as soon as we were born, as soon as we came out of perfection and it still continues—taking us away from the real self and forcing us into the role or wearing the mask that others may think of as you.

On the positive, the conditioning will work for you as long as it serves well for you and everyone else around you. Making your own unaffected choices and decisions is an important aspect of attaining success. So for your own success and well being choose the parts of your conditioning that serve you well. Regardless, you are you and you came here for a reason.

Remember, there are two sides to each story. It is your free will and it is up to you to choose on which side you want to reside—positive or negative, light or dark, giving or receiving, and life or death. You decide!

You have two selves: an outer self and an inner self.

- YOUR OUTER SELF (YOUR PHYSICAL SELF). Your outer self is your body with its organs, tissues, etc., and is visible to the eye. This is the material world where you exist and are most familiar with. In your body, signals are sent from one organ to another through energy.

- YOUR INNER SELF (YOUR SPIRIT). Your inner self cannot be seen but it is felt. The inner self represents the spiritual world and God. It's pure energy.

One of the main reasons we came on Earth is to create light (love, fun, joy, and happiness) in a dark place (the material, egoistic world). It all stems from *The Source of Wealth in You*™—the endless wealth within and God. The connection is missing. When you reconnect your body and mind to the inner Source you will become a conduit to all the riches the universe contains—spiritual and material!

What We Really Want Is Joy and Happiness

And ye shall know the truth, and the truth shall make you free.

THE BIBLE, JOHN 8:32

I personally know that the pain and suffering one keeps going through will continue on until one completes the cycle of birth and death. Simply put, you keep struggling because you have not yet completed the cycle.

This cycle is only complete when you awaken, transform, and correct your current selves and become pure energy that is love. Completion of the cycle of birth and death means total liberation and this is what all of us ultimately want. This is the purpose of going through it all, through many lifetimes, through pain and suffering.

One of the biggest challenges we face daily is to find balance. We came here to bring balance to an out-of-balance world. We live in a dualistic world disturbed physically, emotionally, mentally, and in many other ways as well. However, it's our responsibility to reverse our attitude and actions and make the best of this duality in order to create light. You are a product of your environment but you're also an independent entity. You are free to do anything you choose.

Happiness does not exist in the extremes. Happiness lies toward the center as it aims to achieve that balance. This constant aiming is an art form to be mastered.

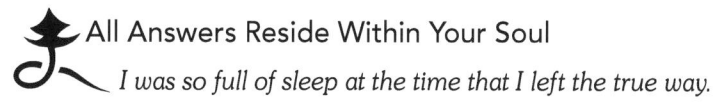

All Answers Reside Within Your Soul

I was so full of sleep at the time that I left the true way.

DANTE ALIGHIERI

To me, the material world is a dream but that's my interpretation and may not necessarily be yours. You came here to make your own reality as part of your mission. On the other hand, the spiritual, unknown world of mystery may be a world only a few know about but everyone can experience and feel.

We come from beauty, perfection, and love. How do I know? Easy answer! Because you keep searching and you want the truth and you know on a deeper level within that there's more to life. It's the truth and the truth is what you want! You know the answers. They're in you, they're in *The Source of Wealth in You*™; I guarantee you.

We're swimming in constant noise in this big material world with all its high tech bells and whistles. Silence is real. The reason most people stay away from silence and surround themselves with noise is because they're simply afraid to be alone and to look within. The truth can be scary, it may hurt, but once you face it, accept it, deal with it and resolve what needs a resolution, the turbulence and confusion will be all over for you. It will open the door to unlimited abundance.

The truth exists within, in your silent world. I do not mean only sitting down with your legs crossed. Silence is wherever you can and want to find it. You can be running while in complete awareness and silence. When you attain an authentic way of existence you'll be naturally tuned in with the universe. Unity represents oneness. When you realize this you have made true spiritual progress. You then truly exist.

A 2007 poll from Newsweek magazine revealed that 91 percent of Americans believe in God and 87 percent identify with a specific religion. One can assume it means that there are millions searching and praying for answers. Why does God answer sometimes and sometimes does not? It depends on your connection with God.

To me, God is energy—the energy that lives within and around us. We're surrounded by God and by His beauty. God is within and the only time you'll get an answer is when you truly communicate with God. God is the Source within, the Source of greatness. God is beauty, peace, calm, happiness and joy. This is the language of God. How sincere and eager are you to learn to speak that language? It's time to get in touch with that part of you, with your inner place of peace and calm. Only then will you be able to reconnect with God.

God has given you a tool to connect with Him—a breath, the breath of life. When you breathe properly you'll start to attain a calmer state of being and you'll become more peaceful—more attuned to yourself and God. When you are in this peaceful state you can speak God's language and God will begin to hear you. You will need to tune in to listen to His answers.

Prayer alone does not always get answered. We are created in a certain way to experience direct contact with God anytime we want. There's a certain way to pray. Become certain that you have the answers within because you're God's creation and God will reveal them to you.

Connect with God right now in this moment: start breathing slowly through your nose from your diaphragm. Witness the flow of air going through your nostrils, in and out; witness your diaphragm moving forward with the inhale and back with the exhale—at the same time. Do just that for a while and make sure the exhale is completed; that is more important than the inhalation! It's important to get rid of the toxins. Soon, your body will naturally begin to relax.

Ask God to hear you. The first thought that comes to you is the truth. Don't question it; just go with that thought. Start talking to God every day. You can only do so by reconnecting with God through your breath and by asking the questions while breathing. This is meditation. Prayer and meditation go together.

In this moment, begin to consciously breathe—to transcend and to enlighten, to become one with God and to end your suffering.

Miracles Will Begin to Appear When You Reconnect with The Source of Wealth in You™—the Unlimited Wealth Within and God

> *Be not afraid of greatness: some are born great, some achieve greatness, and some have greatness thrust upon 'em.*
>
> **SHAKESPEARE (TWELFTH NIGHT)**

You are the most special being ever created! I am too. I am not bragging—just constantly amazed. I had no idea how exceptionally smart, gifted, loving and talented I am until I started to meditate, to practice constant awareness, to take control of my mind and to apply the life-wisdom tools written in this book into my daily life.

I did not know any of this growing up. I come from a dysfunctional family. I was blind to the possibilities within myself. I was a victim of my painful childhood most of which I'd managed to block out of my mind. There were other ways I tried to numb the pain but I'm now certain I survived for a reason. The more awakened I became I discovered what I have already been blessed with—an amazing gift of knowledge and wisdom!

This is *The Source of Wealth in You*™. You have it too; I guarantee you. It will get you through anything you can imagine and beyond. You will rediscover it, reconnect to it and will have it available to you anytime and anywhere when you're finished with this book.

You can only rely on yourself and God. Only when you do you'll never feel insecure again. All you need is to wake up to it. It's a deep well full of wealth that you can draw from endlessly to create anything you need and it will never run dry. The ability to do so is in your hands. It has already been given to you unconditionally. Miracles will begin to appear before your eyes. I experience this every day and I know you can too. You are a free individual; a free human being.

The universe, God, is waiting for you to reclaim your birthright as the greatest magician in the world. You are created with the power to perform real-life miracles. Use the magic wand that you are born with—your breath—to produce the magic show called "My Magical Life" as one that is full of love, joy, peace, bliss, and happiness. Yes, it's that simple: a miraculous life is waiting for you right now.

The Universe Has Been Waiting for You to Align with It

If a man hasn't discovered something that he will die for, he isn't fit to live.

MARTIN LUTHER KING, JR.

Sure, we've all said it: "Why does life have to be so hard?" Or, "Do I have to literally die to make this happen?" Or "will it kill me first?"

The truth is just the opposite: the universe is already perfect! It's simply waiting for you to rediscover perfection within yourself. Why do I claim this is so? If you hadn't already experienced perfection, love, joy, and happiness, why do you keep searching for it? It's because on a deeper level you already know the truth.

My formula for success is to realign yourself with this perfection, with the perfect order in the universe, with God, and to tap into it. It's ready and waiting for you as soon as you are ready to reconnect to it.

When you are balanced, centered, and happy, you will attract the same back to you and success will follow you—you won't have to look for it regardless of what you have previously been taught.

Your arrival on Earth is a success already because you're made of energy, and God is energy, a powerful force. Acknowledge this fact and accept yourself as success already and success will be drawn to you like a magnet. You already have what it takes; it's in each one of you. Dive into the deep waters, into your inner ocean of wonders. You'll be amazed at what is in there; it's the Source of all wealth—the key to a true authentic life of joy and happiness.

I now ask you again to accept these facts in this very moment so you can begin your transformation offered in the following pages and to ultimately return to your pure self and live a meaningful life full of love.

GET STARTED

117 Secrets to Reconnect to Your Divine Power

Knowing yourself is the beginning of all wisdom.

—ARISTOTLE

Make it thy business to know thyself, which is the most difficult lesson in the world.

—MIGUEL DE CERVANTES

Secret 1 | A solid inner foundation is the groundwork for an authentic life.

Contemplation: It is up to you, and you alone, to rebuild the foundation of your life; the foundation from which you exist and operate on a daily basis. But how do you go about rebuilding this foundation? You do it by answering the questions, "Who am I?" What do I believe? (And so on.)

The answers you provide to these questions are strictly individual and only your own answers count for your life. Answer the questions "Who am I?" and "What do I believe?" by reflecting on your core beliefs and values and then putting them down on paper. I also highly recommend that you refer often to what you have written down. Check to make sure that your actions follow your core beliefs. That is the only way to live an authentic life. The fact is that most people do not "walk their talk"—they say one thing and do something else. You do not want to be like that; that's why you're reading this book because you want to be happy. You are looking for authenticity and integration in your life. Happiness and truth go hand-in-hand.

Be very clear and simple about it. Make your life easy and begin today to create light. This is why you came here; to make yourself better and to make this world a better place, to create light—love, joy, and happiness.

Reflect on the following questions:

- What do you think and believe about yourself? Are you a body? A soul? Both? Or perhaps neither?
- What are your core values? Determine five of the values you live by each day and write them down in the space provided.
- What is your life worth to you?
- How do you think you appear to others?
- What do you believe about God? Where does God reside? Within? Around you? Or perhaps nonexistent?
- Where do you operate from? Your soul? Your body? Or something else?
- What is your sense of humor? What makes you laugh?

- How do you see the world you live in? What position do you see it from? Where and how do you fit here, on Earth?

- How willing and capable are you to trust yourself? God? Or something else?

A solid inner foundation is established when you become one with your soul and with God. It's called awareness. Remember to always keep it simple. The first thought that comes into your mind when answering these questions is usually the truest one for you. There are no wrong answers! Write them down and do not overthink—as soon as you start to overthink your mind will start playing games with you!

The Time Is Now! You Have the Answer!
Write the first thought that came to mind and share one action step you will take to create the result you want.   ❧Date: _____

_____

_____

_____

_____

Secret 2 | When the foundation is solid the house can be built.

CONTEMPLATION: Your existence stems from a core, a foundation—*you*. How strong is your spiritual foundation and what is its connection to the world outside of you?

For example, think of your heart, which is such an important part of your body's core, responsible for pumping blood throughout your body and keeping you alive. Suppose one of the heart valves has a blockage and the blood can't pump efficiently. You will not be alive for long. We're connected and exist in unity. In unity—the human body, mind, and soul need to exist. When a disconnection occurs, chaos, pain, suffering, and imbalance will follow. Your connection with God is based on the solidity of your foundation.

Miracles will begin to appear in your life when the ultimate connection happens on the inner and outer level.

- ◆ INNER LEVEL. This is the body-mind-spirit connection—the connection of your body and mind with your soul, and God residing within.
- ◆ OUTER LEVEL. This is your connection with the universe as a whole—the connection of you (the physical self) with God all around you.

If there are cracks in a house's foundation the house will crumble. It will be of no use; it will never shelter a family properly. Using the tools provided here in this book, you will begin to rebuild a solid, strong foundation of truth. Connect to the energy within and unite with the rest of the universe. Take the time to rebuild your inner, soulful foundation. Begin to witness with amazement as the miracles come into your life, one-by-one, to continue rebuilding your strong, eternal home—your life on Earth and beyond. What is waiting for you next is transcendence: an existence at a higher frequency in a higher dimension, eternal freedom, and happiness.

The Time Is Now! You Have the Answer!

Write the first thought that came to mind and share one action step you will take to create the result you want.   DATE:_____

SECRET 3 | Discover an incredible opportunity;
a possibility in each question you have.

CONTEMPLATION: You have lots of questions. Life is a never ending series of questions. Suppose your life was given to you already programmed with everything you need to know and do. What kind of a life would that be? Many people live preprogrammed lives, like robots; never asking questions and accepting everything the way it is given to them. They believe it, live by it, hand it down from generation to generation and eventually die with it. They have lots of questions but they don't bother looking for the answers and the possibilities in the question itself. They just muddle through life somehow.

Why would anyone be satisfied to merely get through life that way? Sadly, some do. There are three types of people: (1) those who are insecure and suffer from low self esteem; (2) those who keep searching and remain on a constant search for the rest of their lives; and (3) those who don't just keep searching and asking the questions but who find (and reveal to themselves and to the world) the incredible opportunities and possibilities that lie in each of the questions they have. The latter is the kind of person we all respect!

To make their lives even more exciting, the third type of people look within and see possibilities in what appears to be seemingly impossible; they discover the opportunity within a question. They get out there and make it happen. These are the people you hear about, admire, and worship. They're fearless and don't doubt themselves. They set their minds on achieving what most people think cannot be achieved and *they do it*.

As I mentioned before, there are always two sides to every coin; similarly, there is a gem to be found in each question you have. For instance, consider the question "Who am I?" It's a simple question and also a profound one. It opens a whole array of other questions and opportunities. Of course, you play certain roles in life—mother, father, wife, husband, daughter, son, and so on, but you are also a lot more than that: you are energy; a soul. You're on the journey of life. And when you think of yourself that way you can see a whole range of other opportunities. Any one of these opportunities can result in you taking a lead to even empower others and to accept your own leadership qualities. There's a leader in each one of you. Only doubt prevents you from taking on a lead role to truly express yourself.

Every question you have is likewise full of meaning, possibilities, and opportunities. Keep asking the questions! Discover the opportunities! Life cannot be taken at face value. You're not an automaton; you're a strong, powerful human being. You're an individual full of inner wealth, ready to reveal yourself to you and to the world!

The Time Is Now! You Have the Answer!

Write the first thought that came to mind and share one action step you will take to create the result you want.   🖋Date:_____

_____

_____

_____

_____

Secret 4 | What you truly need will arrive. It depends solely on your readiness for it.

Contemplation: It has been said that when the student is ready the teacher will appear. Recall that classic line in the movie *Field of Dreams,* "If you build it, they will come." It is so true. When preparations are made, when you are ready, things happen.

Here's an example of how it applied to my life. I spent the summer of 2009 writing this book and I devoted most of my time to it. It felt like a productive summer vacation. I really wanted to complete it and to get my message out. So my life went a bit out of balance, meaning I didn't devote as much of my time to my coaching practice, or to anything else for that matter.

My telephone wasn't ringing that much either, which was good because I was able to focus on my writing. Then September came and the summer was over. I spent a day to get myself back into shape—had my hair trimmed and colored, got a manicure and pedicure, etc. The moment I was ready, refreshed and looking great, my phone started ringing. The phone calls were from people who I hadn't heard from or met with for over a year; now, they suddenly wanted to get together, wanted to see what I'm doing and to even do some business together. It was fruitful! This is a simple example of taking action to get ready for what is to come into your life; witness how your readiness actually materializes new events.

The moment you get yourself ready, your dreams start to materialize. Are you ready?

The Time Is Now! You Have the Answer!
Write the first thought that came to mind and share one action step you will take to create the result you want.   ❥Date: _____

_____

_____

_____

_____

Secret 5 | Meditation will take you home to your true nature that is love.

CONTEMPLATION: Meditation is not concentration or contemplation. You need not to focus on anything; it's about *being*. You're just being you. Many people don't want to meditate because they think it'll become boring when you have to focus and concentrate.

At first, like anything that's worth your time, witnessing your breath and diaphragm at the same time will feel new to you and bit unusual. But here's the key: I don't support methods and techniques that make people work hard. I started that way but now I've learned how to tailor to my own specific needs certain methods and techniques that are easy and effective.

I also have discovered that some of my practices awaken my natural eroticism and that feels amazing, a never ending sense of pleasure. Can you imagine that—just sitting by yourself experiencing intense sexual pleasure? Sounds fun, right? This is what meditation is—it's fun; it's sexy.

When I meditate I get chills; my body jerks, or it gets really heated. Often, my body feels weightless, or I encounter faces I've never seen before and it feels good inside and physically too. Wow, I'm on an adventure!

Meditation really is fun. Please, remember this word—*fun*. I am all about that. Anything that feels like work to me does not work for me. When my friend Ellen asked me, "What are you doing for the Fourth of July?" I said, "Oh, nothing—meditating." I mentioned this to my friend Sam and he burst out laughing. He thinks it's funny that I find such joy in meditation!

Begin a daily connection with yourself. Practice going to bed and getting up early especially before the sun comes up. Be the first one to wake up and take charge of your life. The rest of the world is asleep. Why can't you be the one who is up early making a difference in the world? You're different, right? Practice what I call THE SOURCE OF WEALTH IN YOU™ MEDITATION©.

THE SOURCE OF WEALTH IN YOU™ MEDITATION©

THE SOURCE OF WEALTH IN YOU™ MEDITATION© is a state of being without concentration, thoughts, effort, or focusing of the mind. It consists of conscious and proper breathing. You will become aware of the present moment and will connect to your Higher Self, the universal intelligence, God, as a way of life. Simply begin to breathe from your diaphragm while witnessing both—the stream of air going in and out of your nostrils simultaneously with the inhale/exhale of your diaphragm (expanding out with the inhale and going back in with the exhale). Always breathe through your nose and give a nice long exhale. When it becomes second nature to you, you can consciously exist through this technique. Until then, choose the setting and position that personally suits you best.

Give yourself and others the gift of meditation. Practice daily until conscious breathing becomes part of your existence. When you meditate regularly you'll eventually start to feel love inside of you, and once you feel it, you will start giving and receiving it too. Until then, you're living a life that might be a dream for all we know—an illusion. In this dream, you will be in constant need of love and you won't find it; I guarantee it. Even when you think you have found it, it won't last long and you will be back to where you started—back to looking for love. *Become love and you will attract the same—love.*

The Time Is Now! You Have the Answer!
Write the first thought that came to mind and share one action step you will take to create the result you want.   ❥Date:_____

_____

_____

_____

_____

Secret 6 | Believing in yourself is a sure way to happiness.

CONTEMPLATION: People doubt themselves. Feeling insecure is related to low self esteem but also to your environment. It has nothing to do with your true authentic self—your spirit—and God.

For example, I have a friend I'll call Alan whose whole existence is completely affected by the outside world. When he was laid off from work he spent most of his time at home where he had no extra stimulus and felt more peaceful. As soon as he took a job he started feeling a sense of insecurity and pressure to fit in because he was motivated by external influences. In the meantime, he kept changing his mind about who he felt he was and what he wanted to do with his life. Every time we spoke he had a different version of his life's direction: from going to college, to traveling around the world, to living with his family until the economy improved.

Alan is affected by outside influences and does not operate from his Source. This is what happens when you doubt yourself. You accept whatever gets thrown at you instead of becoming the co-creator of your life and standing strong on your own feet. Believe in yourself because insecurity is just like cancer—a hard-to-cure disease—it will eat you up alive sometimes without you even realizing it. Live your life with a belief in yourself, with certainty, and you'll attract certainty.

True belief comes from *you* not from somewhere else. If you are carrying baggage from your past and upbringing, it's not really yours; it was given to you—discard it. People who believe in themselves accomplish wonders. To use myself as an example, I have always known somehow that no matter what I go through, eventually everything will work out for me. I know it's the same for you, too. Think about it! To make life a little easier, it really helps to have someone to talk to, such as teacher, mentor, or a life coach. It makes a huge difference. This is how I discovered the power of motivation. Every time I felt motivated by someone I achieved wonders.

However, you cannot count on other people or get addicted to outside sources of motivation. Count on yourself. The more you believe and don't doubt yourself, the sooner your energy, full of certainty, will attract similar kind of energy.

The Time Is Now! You Have the Answer!
Write the first thought that came to mind and share one action step you will take to create the result you want.   🖋DATE: _____

_____

_____

_____

Secret 7 | All you need is love. Love is energy.

CONTEMPLATION: Love is essential to your life and success. The absence of it can literally destroy your life. People who lead lives full of love are successful and happy. They also look and feel younger than the rest. I want to share with you the story of one of the people who came to me for help.

Henry is forty two years old but he looks significantly older. He has spent most of his life alone and he shared with me his belief that he is a coward. Henry is a good man and has learned some great lessons in life but he has surrendered to his past wounds and still carries the baggage. His dad died when he was two years old and he was raised by his single mom. He didn't have a father figure which is very important in a boy's life.

Henry let the past affect his whole life. Fear has been his leading motivator. Currently, he suffers from diabetes, heart disease, and joint pain causing his body to ache. Henry seems to have had a lifetime of pain. He also was married once for five years and his wife became pregnant but had a miscarriage.

Can you see how the imprint of your past affects your current life? Can you see how fear and regret can poison your whole existence? Henry has lived a life of fear and that simply attracted more fear and misfortune into his life. How could his marriage have had any other outcome? Today, at only forty two, Henry is afraid of love and of becoming a father. The unhealed unhappiness of his childhood led directly to his short lived marriage and subsequent divorce, as well as to his development of some serious physical illnesses.

Can you see the thread that entwines itself throughout a human life? In life, misfortunes happen, but it is your responsibility to resolve the past and to move on before it debilitates your whole existence. Responsibility requires maturity but most people take a long time to mature—often half their lives! Many are unwilling to mature and they cling to irresponsibility like a baby clings to a pacifier.

Physical illness is the result of stagnated energy in one or more of your energy bodies (aka the human energy field or aura). Remember, you are made of energy. The solution for my client is the energy of love. He is missing love from his life. He didn't have love when he was little, which wasn't his fault, but he has kept on going without love until today. Henry is not aware of himself; he seems almost to have been sleepwalking through life. At times, during our sessions, he has appeared to wake up—and what a wonderful thing that has been to see! But it's a bit difficult for him to stick to a new routine with new habits because he has lived a loveless life and he's used to it. Henry has a lot more work to do. He will not attract love into his life until he purifies and heals his past, his energy, his thoughts, his whole being and begins to love himself.

I encourage people to work on themselves. Begin to meditate as soon as possible. When you start a personal development daily routine early in life there will be a lot less baggage to lose. The longer you've lived, the more baggage you've accumulated.

You are a physical body made of and surrounded by energy. The energy cannot be seen but felt—and that's God. God is love; love heals; love is energy.

The Time Is Now! You Have the Answer!
Write the first thought that came to mind and share one action step you will take to create the result you want.   ✎Date:

SECRET 8 | The Principle of Restriction© will bring miracles into your life.

CONTEMPLATION: I want to share an example that made me extremely proud of myself, especially as it relates to my personal development journey. Jacob is a business professional with whom I was looking forward to partner up to work on wellness projects. Unfortunately, our relationship did not work out. We were not a good match as a business team. While I was working on developing a new website, I kept Jacob's photo and credentials on my previous website. One day, I received a nasty phone call from Jacob's assistant insisting that I remove Jacob's information from my website immediately.

I was on the verge of exploding because of the nasty tone in her voice. Almost immediately, I remembered what I discovered and experimented with—the PRINCIPLE OF RESTRICTION©. I restricted myself from reacting to her attitude and I took a few deep slow breaths and removed Jacob's info from my website as asked. Then I started thinking about him.

Since I knew Jacob very well I figured he was going through one of his daily emotional breakdowns. He didn't call me himself because he did not have the guts but did it in a mean and underhanded way through his assistant. I managed to overcome my irritation in the quiet of my room. I focused on my positive energy to send Jacob some good thoughts. Sure enough, Jacob felt my energy and it obviously made him feel guilty. But that was not my intention. For the next two days I kept receiving phone calls from his office, from his assistant.

I called Jacob back. Suddenly, while talking to him I shared a family emergency issue I was dealing with that had just come up. And, lo-and-behold, Jacob reached in like a magician pulling out a white rabbit. Out of nowhere he proposed a resolution to my problem and helped me bring my family matter to a quick conclusion. All of this happened as a result of my application of what I discovered and named the PRINCIPLE OF RESTRICTION©.

Principle of Restriction©

The mind, the ego, has a tendency to mislead you, to overreact. It's possible that you may react in a way that can cause irreparable damage. Take control of your mind, restrict your reactions, and remain calm and peaceful at all times.

Because I took the time to tune in to my soul and to the positive energy that I am and reacted with the opposite (the reverse) of what Jacob, his assistant and even I expected, I turned a tricky situation into a peaceful resolution, and it worked out for the best.

First, I kept Jacob as a dear friend and most importantly, by restricting myself from exploding during one of his moody days I allowed light to enter between us. I had no idea that Jacob would even get involved with the personal issue I was dealing with at the time but he did, and a major resolution in my life took place.

This is a crystal clear example of how my soul, my inner Source of Truth, my subconscious already had the answers within, before I was even aware of it. This is *The Source of Wealth in You*™ I am writing this book about. The trick to life is to always react, act, and exist from the Source of Wealth within before your emotions take over. I urge you to reconnect to and operate from the Source exclusively. I guarantee you success!

The Time Is Now! You Have the Answer!
Write the first thought that came to mind and share one action step you will take to create the result you want.   DATE:_____

Resolve The Past; Remain in the Present

I count him braver who overcomes his desires
than him who overcomes his enemies.

—Aristotle

Secret 9 | If your past causes you to suffer today, accept and release it now and forever.

CONTEMPLATION: Your physical body is surrounded by layers of energy called energy bodies (aka the human energy field or aura). If you want to become happier and to succeed in life, release the trauma from the past stored in your energy bodies through an energy-based healing method, one of the few mentioned in the Glossary. Holding onto a poisonous energy accumulated from the past within the energy bodies will eventually manifest into a physical illness within the body, such as stroke, heart attack, depression, anxiety, and many other dis-eases.

You live life and make decisions in the present based on your past experiences. But if you hold onto the so-called painful past it will destroy your life today. It will prevent you from moving ahead and from looking at any new situation with a different perspective.

Human beings are masters at forgetting—it's how we're structured. Honestly, the ability to forget is part of who you are. Can you imagine yourself remembering everything? When you want to remember a lot of information, when you study, it's information overload; our brains can only remember enough to keep us from "going crazy." So it's natural for you to forget, and that includes forgetting your past. In fact, I suggest to simply resolve it and release the memory because trying to forget what remains unresolved in your soul will come back to haunt you later.

Consider the past and the psychic baggage you've been carrying around as a result of it and then release it. Bid it "adieu." Just keep the lessons you've learned from it. Be on a constant watch and remain consciously aware of the fact that as soon as you bring in trash from the past, you'll damage the experience you're going through in the present, right now. Train yourself to be able to discern what is useful from the past and what is not.

Complete balance does not exist on Earth. But the actual striving toward balance between the two opposites you're presented with each day is what makes life worth living. So accept the process and consciously release the past because it's over and is keeping you stuck. Remind yourself each day so it becomes a habit.

Remember, memories of who you were or what happened in the past will only twist your version of the present because a lot of your past experiences came into your life as lessons, just for you to learn from. Learning may seem unpleasant in the beginning, especially what you resist. Why do you think most kids hate going to school? So, if there's trauma to release from your past, or from growing up, try reliving your childhood! Go back and re examine the past. The following is a fun and rewarding exercise that I call I Release My Past Meditation©.

I Release My Past Meditation©

Take an unpleasant incident from your past and see it as though it's a movie clip or something you're watching on TV or YouTube. Choose only one three minute clip. Imagine yourself standing up on a tall building or even up in the sky so you can watch yourself in the scene below from above. It does not matter where you are, as long as you can watch yourself as though you're an "actor" playing a particular character in it, not a participant. Repeat the scene of the incident slowly from beginning to end; step-by-step, over-and-over as it happened. Watch yourself in it until you've watched it many times. After awhile you'll find that the situation isn't yours anymore and you can detach from it as easy as you could from something you saw on TV.

When you begin to watch yourself as a witness, as opposed to feeling that you're still living in it though it's already gone, you will begin to slowly release the trauma from the past. You'll be on your way to "the now." The past will turn into something you only witnessed and you're now detached from; it will not belong to you anymore. You'll be able to say, "I've seen this clip a thousand times. It's not all that interesting and I don't want to watch it anymore." Remember to watch yourself in that moment of your life—in that event. Do not participate in it but consciously witness it.

Because you're learning to let go of your past, you'll want to make living in the present fun as well. Life is truly a game. You cannot take it too seriously.

So begin to play life as a game and make it your strategy to let go of the past. If the damage is too deep to release, find a professional energy healer or therapist to help you heal and release the painful energy you've been holding. What a relief it will be!

The Time Is Now! You Have the Answer!
Write the first thought that came to mind and share one action step you will take to create the result you want.   **Date:** _____

_____

_____

_____

_____

Secret 10 | Unresolved life issues will turn into physical illness.

Contemplation: Your physical health depends on how freely and effectively the energy you are made of flows through your physical body. Additionally, the connection of your own energy with the universal energy, God, is of major importance. When there's an energy block, your physical body will start ailing—which you may be unaware of until you become sick.

There is a constant exchange of energy. The body has a natural need to release its own energy and to receive energy as well. It flows both ways—just as the tides come in and out, just as the moon waxes and wanes, and just as night becomes day.

A clear example of our need to release and to receive energy is when we make love. The energy exchange we experience from making love nourishes our souls. Another example of an outward release is the experience of an orgasm. It's a healthy release that we need but it must come naturally from within, in the form of love, not from a technique you use to calm yourself down.

Another example deals with the emotion of anger. Certainly anger needs to be released but in a constructive way. Holding onto anger will eventually turn into an emotional illness, which will manifest into a physical illness. On the other hand, when you make someone angry, the "polluted" energy they subconsciously reflect back at you will cause you emotional suffering and illness as well. So by all means, become aware of these facts so you don't have to wonder what happened or why you feel irritated.

Unresolved past or current issues will cause you both physical and emotional pain. Resolve the unresolved that still resides in your energy bodies, both from the past and present. One of the best ways to resolve it is to gather up your courage and to face it. An open, honest communication with yourself or another is a must.

I am amazed at how often people ignore the issues. *Not facing what has to be faced and then released in order to move on with your life is what's making you sick!* Remember, we live in a material world; here, our souls walk around in physical bodies that are full of unreleased emotional baggage. This unreleased and unresolved energy from that baggage keeps you stuck and weighs you down.

Here's an example from my life: When I first discovered meditation as the way to my existence, I started to meditate a great deal. It felt good because on the surface my life was running smoothly, yet I was still somehow feeling uncomfortable on the inside. I was also attracting certain kinds of people, especially those who drained my energy, even from a distance. I began to feel overwhelmed and unable to do much; I couldn't even work. So I went to an energy healer who discovered three interesting things: (1) Because I had meditated, I was becoming very spiritually advanced, but I still had some old baggage, pain, and trauma from childhood that I had not yet released, so there were energy blocks I still had within. In other words, I was getting way ahead of myself! (2) My chakras were out of balance, so an energy healer helped me to balance them out. (3) My root chakra was so charged up that I was attracting men sexually like a magnet. I was not operating from my heart chakra, which emanates love, and this is why the men I kept attracting were emotionally blocked themselves!

You must take care of yourself to live a meaningful life. Recognize what is draining or blocking your energy, and then deal with it, *right now*. If you're tired, lifeless and unhappy it is simply because you have not taken care of yourself. You can turn that around easier than you think—so start today!

The Time Is Now! You Have the Answer!

Write the first thought that came to mind and share one action step you will take to create the result you want. ✐Date:

___

Secret 11 | How I transformed myself and became the Source of light.

CONTEMPLATION: The very words "change" and "transformation" sound a bit daunting and even difficult and complicated. However, we change all the time but just don't quite realize it; everything in our world moves so quickly, we can "change" five times in one way or another before we realize something in us has even occurred! Human nature works like this: human beings are all insecure on some level; they want attention; they need to love and to be loved; they act and react according to their insecurities.

Here's an example from my own life. A few years ago, I was very insecure and desperately looking for love and attention. So I acted a bit weird and not all together. It was an act, a role I played to get what I wanted at the time—love and attention. I played this role for a while but it didn't lead me anywhere; it didn't bring me the love and attention I so direly needed at the time. The result was the opposite; it turned people off! In addition, I was going through lots of emotional pain, turmoil, suffering, drama, and depression. Who wants to be around that, right?

Then I started the search; a journey that I took mostly through the vehicle of meditation; three years later I discovered and experimented with what I named the PRINCIPLE OF THE OPPOSITE ACTION©.

PRINCIPLE OF THE OPPOSITE ACTION©

We live in a world of opposites, dualities and dichotomies: male/female, good/bad, yin/yang, and positive/negative. We struggle with these dichotomies each day. I knew the material world is a tough, dark place but I also took into consideration that I came here to make this world a better place and to create light.

How can one create light? Think about a simple electric circuit or a flashlight battery; it takes two opposite poles, the positive and the negative, to create light. When I thought about that I knew that if I kept adding to all the negativity in an already negative world I couldn't create light. I needed two opposites.

When I came up with this idea it felt amazing; and it felt equally amazing to put it into action! I deliberately went against the negative side of my nature and acted contrary to the way I used to normally act. The results were almost startling. I was creating light by connecting the negativity I encountered out in the world with my positive nature. Try it for yourself and see what happens! You'll be astonished too!

The Time Is Now! You Have the Answer!
Write the first thought that came to mind and share one action step you will take to create the result you want. DATE:_____

SECRET 12 | Let go of the past; it's gone anyway.

CONTEMPLATION: Renewal is happiness and change is necessary in order to renew. Change is constant; it's a natural occurrence. Letting go is a must in order to renew yourself and your life. Letting go can be as simple as getting your hair trimmed and cutting off the dead ends. Your hair will look thick and healthy; you will look and feel better, even younger. But to consciously and willingly let go of "things"—that can be hard! Most people have cluttered homes because there are so many beautiful things out there to buy and you seem to want to have more. This is how people fill the void within, by bringing in more clutter into their lives.

It can be hard to let go because of the sentimental value and memories. But when a disaster occurs such as an earthquake, fire, tornado or flood that ruins a houseful of prized possessions, people are forced to start a new life. At first, of course, it's a huge blow to their system, but there are no "accidents." Perhaps some of them "needed" a natural disaster to make a change within and to get rid of what they didn't need anymore. When you don't take charge of your life in the areas in which it needs to be readjusted, the universe will naturally step in and do it for you! There is a perfect order, a perfect universe.

When the initial shock and period of mourning begins to wear off, people often feel as though they've been ushered into a new beginning and they will begin to feel a sense of cleansing and renewal, almost rejuvenation, because they no longer have what they needed to let go.

But how can you start over without waiting for a disaster? If you want to bring clarity and renewal, take a look at what you have and let only the things with the most special value stay with you.

Create space in your home and within your heart to allow a perfect flow of renewed energy to enter into your life. Clear your mental obstacles by getting rid of physical clutter. And how about the old destructive relationships you've collected? Some of them are suffocating your life. What are you going to do to reverse the affect they have on you?

What can you let go of today? I guarantee you that once you do, the new will soon take its place that's likely to be more suited to the present stage of your life.

The Time Is Now! You Have the Answer!
Write the first thought that came to mind and share one action step you will take to create the result you want.   ✒ DATE: _____

_____

_____

_____

_____

SECRET 13 | Become aware of what your soul needs, not what your body wants.

CONTEMPLATION: There's so much happening out there, our heads can spin. There's a lot of information; items to buy; new fashions coming out every day; electronic gadgets…enough to make us crazy! As soon as you purchased a great CD player, the MP3s came in, then you bought an MP3 player, but newer models started coming out—cheaper, more compact, and powerful. Then the iPod showed up and new cell phones; the iPhone; more-compact computers, TVs too cool to resist; the list can go on and on …the "stuff" doesn't end!

That's because it's all focused on the product buyers, on marketing models and on consumers, but not on you—the individual. Anything outside of your soul, that which exists in the material world is where temporary happiness resides. Life on Earth is designed in such a way as to keep your attention outside of yourself. This explains why it's a challenge to focus on the inside.

You are the star of this lifetime. The manufacturers need you to buy their products but you don't have to participate in their marketing plan. It's not your problem so don't make it your "business!" You're free to stay focused on yourself—on your own sanity, joy, happiness, and self-knowledge. All the outside chaos is probably making you unhappy anyway, isn't it? It makes you want and it makes you covet. How unhealthy for your soul! I know it makes me unhappy—because I can't afford to buy all I want. How can I? I want it all! And my mind can't take it anymore, so it loses control and I start to feel like I'm bereft and less than, or needful of things that I don't even want! It's a crazy, endless cycle!

Do you still wonder why you're unhappy? A life based on materialism is like a dangling carrot that we can't have. You're asleep to the truth and you can't think straight. You're being controlled by the influence of brilliant marketing. Don't give in to the lure of consumerism. Your soul needs more than this. To create peace and fulfillment, begin to apply what I named the PRINCIPLE OF SELECTIVE DESIRE©.

PRINCIPLE OF SELECTIVE DESIRE©

Life is a series of choices; anything you do or don't do is your choice. Your happiness depends on the choices you make! You can easily select which of your desires to pursue because you're free to do so. You're a human being graciously imbued with free will.

To become a contributor and to change the world, get in touch with the real you and carefully select and make choices—what to let in, what to keep out, and what you know and feel is best for you. Beware of your mind and your ego's desires! Who is running you? You are the only one who has the power to take charge of your life.

The Time Is Now! You Have the Answer!
Write the first thought that came to mind and share one
action step you will take to create the result you want.   **DATE:** _____

SECRET 14 | Addictions will block the perfect energy flow of happiness.

CONTEMPLATION: Because you're human, you're attracted and attached to drama, confusion, pain, and suffering. You're addicted to the negative memories and experiences from the past because they are familiar, and the familiar brings comfort, as crippling as they may be. You go on with your life without even realizing you're holding on to negative energy. Yet, at the same time, you struggle to release the pain and suffering because you want to be happy. You keep fighting within yourself between the two opposites: the good and the bad, and the positive and the negative. It seems hard to balance them.

A complete balance does not exist in the material world and that's the way it's supposed to be. Imagine yourself living in a perfect material world. Life in a perfect material world would not be life at all; in fact, it would be really boring! Life on Earth is about the action you take. It's about the aiming toward balance to reach middle ground between the two opposites. This is what makes life fulfilling.

Your daily challenge is to overcome suffering because it's physically and emotionally draining. You want to enjoy life and be happy, but you're stuck with pain. You keep torturing yourself. Why do you keep doing this to yourself? It's because this is what you know how to do well. When you realize this reality and become aware of your thoughts, mind, ego, and behavior, you'll start moving into a different zone and into higher inner and outer energy levels. You'll begin to let go of the comfort of sabotaging your own happiness.

Transformation and the new way of living your life may feel uncomfortable only because you're not used to it. You're used to constant confusion now, so when the issues start clearing out, it will feel awkward or perhaps empty until you learn to fill yourself with light. It's like when a wish does come true, you may not know what to do with it. But as in anything you do with any amount of real practice, one day you'll notice your life has changed and you'll feel happier.

Be patient with yourself while you're getting used to the new way of living and moving toward a happier state of being. This is the beginning of so much more to come. You're finding your way to *The Source of Wealth in You*™. When you begin to notice the discomfort, know that it is a stepping stone to the happiness that awaits you.

The Time Is Now! You Have the Answer!
Write the first thought that came to mind and share with me one action step you will take to create the result you want.   **Date:** _____

_____

_____

_____

_____

Secret 15 | When you come from a place of need, your life is guaranteed to turn into a mess.

Contemplation: Your understanding and acceptance of the following two facts will bring in and work miracles in your life: (1) the universe is abundant, and (2) you are abundance.

Think of the gift of being human, born here, on Earth. How awakened are you to this gift given to you by God? Most people are not awakened to it at all; indeed, they are blind to it. What is preventing people from seeing the truth? They're not connected to their true nature, to *The Source of Wealth in You*™. When one is connected to this Source and operates from it, one can clearly see, know, feel, and draw endlessly from the abundance within. Conversely, coming from a place of need would bring unnecessary events into your life.

Before my awakening, a few years ago, I met a man I'll call Michael. Though I was communicating my attraction to him on a soul level, quite the opposite was occurring on a physical level—I was denying to myself and to him the attraction I thought I had for him! How complicated is that, right? But he could feel it all no matter how much I denied it.

Michael is great at what he does in his profession, so I was attracted to that too. It had absolutely nothing to do with the love! What a complete mess! My energy was strong and I became a magnet for all the wrong reasons. And to top it all off, he was emotionally unavailable anyway because he was already in a long term intimate relationship.

We started arguing because my ego kept denying the truth. Everything became unbelievably chaotic because I also woke up to something else: the realization that I needed Michael for my own selfish reasons! I was operating out of my desperation, from a place of need. I needed Michael more than anything else. Actually, later I remembered that when I first met him I wasn't really attracted to him physically; that only came later.

The rest was a series of disappointments, misunderstandings and arguments. My whole encounter with Michael was all so complicated—and all due to my neediness. I needed him, yes, on some, shall we say, "mind/ego" level. I found myself even fantasizing about partnering up with him and having a successful family business. Yet all of that led to my so called physical attraction to someone who wasn't even available.

At that time, I hadn't yet awakened to the fact that I have all I need to succeed in life. Yes, we as human beings do need each other, but not when we come from a place of neediness, desperation, selfishness, and dependency.

Make sure to always ask yourself, what place am I coming from in my dealings with this person? From my heart? From my desire to control? From physical attraction? Or from what else? We have the Source within. That's true abundance. It's the Source of unlimited wealth. How can we let ourselves forget that?

The Time Is Now! You Have the Answer!

Write the first thought that came to mind and share one action step you will take to create the result you want.   **Date:** _____

_____

_____

_____

_____

Secret 16 | Life is beautiful. Contribute to its beauty through conscious control of your addictions.

Contemplation: Most human beings have some sort of addiction. Addictions are part of life here in the material world, and they can also be interpreted as part of nature's balancing act, pulling the left and the right extremes toward the middle where balance and happiness are found.

Addiction, however, does not always have a negative connotation. Learn to recognize this life rule: There isn't such a thing as good or bad within God's boundaries. What is good or bad depends solely on your interpretations and beliefs. Life is about finding the balance between the two.

People live unbalanced lives. Now, living a bit on the edge will release the baggage from the inside out. It depends on what your description of "living on the edge" is, but as long as you're not hurting anyone, it's fine.

The nature of life is about change, action, transformation, and constant movement. You can clearly see it in the way your moods change. Spend some time with your moods to start recognizing the flux and flow of them. Whenever you find yourself in what you may think of as a bad mood, just give it some time; a little later you'll find yourself in a completely different mood.

(I am talking about healthy mood fluctuation here and not about unhealthy mood imbalances and extremes.)

It's the same with your addictions, visible or not; they come, they go, or stay. I recently met Alex, who seems to be addicted to the ecstatic moments of life. I told him that this kind of addiction would bring him lots of disappointments. I also told him that as he learned how to consciously tune in to the natural flow of universal energy, he would begin to accept the fact that there would naturally be downtime after every great moment. In addition, I felt he needed to become aware of and realize the temporary nature of the downtime and life events in general. Once Alex accepted this fact, he was prepared to (1) get through his next disappointment more easily; and (2) shift his energy and become a catalyst in transforming the negative energy of any event into positive energy by readjusting and altering his own energy more quickly toward the positive, thus attracting it sooner.

Save yourself from unhappiness by accepting the evidence of impermanence on Earth. I call this practice "mind control." Good mind control requires awareness of the human addictions.

The Time Is Now! You Have the Answer!
Write the first thought that came to mind and share one action step you will take to create the result you want.   DATE:_____

SECRET 17 | The highest form of personal power is to completely surrender your desire to control.

CONTEMPLATION: How many people have you met who have no desire to control? None, right? Why is that? Because control is the ego's favorite form of expression. Humans have different ways of expressing that desire. Some are expressive and loud about it, and some are subtle.

Why is the desire to control so strong in humans? It comes from the very crux of your ego, which likes to think it's important. Some may think if I let that go, then I will become "nobody"—without identity and without a sense of self. Humans try so hard to control the things outside of themselves but lose the focus and ability to control their own selves.

The reality of true control lies in the opposite direction. The truest sort of control is control of ourselves, and actually, that is the only sort of control we have. It is the ultimate form of control.

How can we attain full control of ourselves? Reduce the noise in your life from the outside world. You may protest, saying that you can't find time. I disagree. Instead of participating in group activities which satisfy your sense of belonging from a psychological point of view, begin a new activity today. Set aside some time to spend alone, completely quiet; to breathe, and to listen to yourself breathe. Your inner voice, your inner Source of Wealth, will reveal itself to you if you have patience to spend some time alone, to breathe and to listen.

This is real power; the power to listen and to connect to the Source—your soul and God residing within. The rest happens in the form of miracles, and it will come to you. There is no need to look for it, but to connect with *The Source of Wealth in You*™. It means connecting to God because God is the Source too. You are the Source because God is within you. *It all happens through breathing and listening.*

The Time Is Now! You Have the Answer!
Write the first thought that came to mind and share one action step you will take to create the result you want. 🌿**Date:** _____

SECRET 18 | Desperation cripples human existence. Letting go of your desperation will open the energy flow to receive.

CONTEMPLATION: "The mass of men lead lives of quiet desperation," wrote Thoreau. "What is called resignation is confirmed desperation." Do you ever feel that way—resigned, desperate, stuck in a rut from which you just can't seem to dig yourself out of?

Desperation is a form of extreme desire. Determine the root of your desires so that you won't fall into a frustrated life of resignation or desperation. People often feel powerless because they limit themselves; in other words, they've given away their power—they've willingly handcuffed themselves to an ever turning wheel.

That ever turning wheel is society. Society decrees that there are certain rules and regulations we must follow. But do we have to follow blindly, in a way that is unacceptable, a way that makes our lives hardly worth living? I'm certain that your answer will be "no!" Otherwise, you would not be seeking happiness. You would not be reading this book.

It isn't easy to free yourself and that is why most people do not do it. They are filled with fear. For example, because they feel responsible for the well being of their family, they remain at the same secure job with benefits their whole life and all of that time they remain unhappy.

If you are in that situation, recognize it. Ask yourself if that is really what you want to do with your life. And ask your family members too, because it's likely that they have sensed your inner turmoil and unhappiness, and it has made them unhappy too to see you this way. If you feel good about your life and remove yourself from a life of quiet desperation, your family and everyone around you will become happier and inspired too. They will admire you and will see that they too have free will and are not doomed to live the way someone else thinks they should.

In the space provided, write your answers to the following questions:

- ◆ You seem to hold on to people, events, the past, etc., in despair. Why? What do you gain from it?

- ◆ You desperately want certain things—a better job, a house, a soulmate, a high definition television, etc.—and can't stop pushing yourself and others to get what you want. You keep wanting more. Have you ever asked yourself why?

- ◆ You want others, your kids, your partner to change, to do things your way, but it doesn't seem to work. Let them be who they are. They will begin to notice the freedom they have to express their own individuality and will change of their own accord. Why do you want others to change?

Everything is interconnected and each desire you have and each action you take will affect everyone else. When you're desperate you will cause an energy outage. It's like when you overload the circuits in your house—when you plug in three electric heaters and turn them on full blast because you're desperate to heat the house.

Desperation affects your physical body: it flips your inner circuit breakers and the energy flow is cut off. It halts the continual ongoing transformation of who you truly are. Releasing your desperation will allow you to open up and be able to determine what is holding you back. When you let go of your desperation what you truly need will suddenly appear. It's part of the balancing act of nature. Allow for what you need to naturally come into your life!

The Time Is Now! You Have the Answer!
Write the first thought that came to mind and share one action step you will take to create the result you want.   ♪Date:_____

SECRET 19 | When you stop thinking about the future your real life can begin.

CONTEMPLATION: Constant change, exchange of energy, never ending movement, changing tides of life events—this is life! How do you fit all this constant change into your own transformation? The true question is—how do you not fit it in?

Human lives are to be lived with meaning. Human beings need to reconnect to pure happiness. Isn't that what you strive to achieve daily, beyond survival? Because there is constant change in life, which is part of nature, become consciously aware of the instability of your thoughts about the future. How can you possibly know the future when nature always takes its own course?

I want to remind you of two really important facts:

- The closer you are to nature, the more you become a natural part of its course. I call this being "in tune."

- You're naturally striving toward balance, toward the middle where true happiness lies. To move closer toward balance (depending on the situation you're in) apply the PRINCIPLE OF THE OPPOSITE ACTION©.

Anything that feels hard for you and what you resist is usually good for you! To execute this principle, simply counteract your "human" tendencies, desires, etc., with what you don't feel like doing or acting upon, always within God's boundaries. Enjoy the results from a daily conscious application of this principle! Stretch your wings; take a risk; try anything that will get you out of your comfort zone of your unfulfilling life. Consider the rules of order in the material world, but practice and experience balance by bringing the two opposites (the negative and the positive) toward the middle.

Remain in the present moment. Recognize and catch yourself every time a disturbing thought, usually about the past or the future, comes in and distracts you. Why? Because that thought is taking you away from "the now," and it is a ruse, a lure set out by your mind to keep you away from your own reality.

This disturbing thought is taking you to a fantasyland and into the future. When you start thinking about the future, you become stuck there, worried or fantasizing about what may never even happen! It's like borrowing trouble!

In the meantime, while you're thinking about your future, the universal energy in the present has shifted. When you neglect to remind yourself about this constant change and movement, you become stuck in daydreams and fantasies. Then you get attached to them. Then you become frustrated because you didn't consider the constant change of nature as part of the future; you didn't allow yourself to factor that in. When you do, however, all your worries about the "unknown future" will cease!

The Time Is Now! You Have the Answer!
Write the first thought that came to mind and share one action step you will take to create the result you want.   **Date:** _____

_____

_____

_____

_____

Secret 20 | The present moment is your only refuge from a painful past or unrealistic expectations about the future.

Contemplation: The expression "living in the now" is hot out there. Everyone is talking about it. I personally think it's impossible to live in the present moment as long as your mind interferes. You carry emotional baggage with you too. How do you shed it? There are so many theories, but they're only that—theories.

Theories and philosophies are of no use to me because everyone has them. Talk is cheap. In addition to learning how to control your mind, and to practice it constantly, set a specific goal and take three action steps toward it. There are teachings and gurus that tell you to not do anything and let life develop naturally. Absolutely, things are best when developed naturally but not through waiting. There's a very insidious, thin line between the two, so make sure you don't get the two tangled up. "Developing naturally" implies action, whereas, "waiting for life to develop naturally" implies passivity.

You just can't wait on anything in life. If you don't get on with it, you're blocking the natural progress of life. Simply initiate action, whatever it may be. Even if you're not sure what action to take, I urge you to still take a small step to get the ball rolling! Just a simple move on your part will open up the energy flow with tons of possibilities.

Have you noticed that when you don't know what to do with your life, if you get out there and get even just a part-time job, it eventually leads to more opportunities and the answers start to reveal themselves? Action is the answer. More precisely, balance between action and stillness is the answer!

Take action, but don't ignore the daily connection with your soul, with God, in silence, in meditation. Stillness is the opposite of action, but it's also the opposite of "waiting." Stillness is a must in order to bring the two together—action (the positive) and waiting (the negative)—to move toward the middle, toward balance. Apply the PRINCIPLE OF THE OPPOSITE ACTION© daily. Become a vehicle of even, continuous, balanced motion. Consciously support your vehicle's natural course toward an authentic development of events.

Remember, when your actions are in alignment with your soul, your life and existence will become effortless. For instance, certain people are always on the go, often complaining that they are extremely busy and that they can never stop. Some are in manic episodes trying to get to the future—or at least catch a glimpse of it before it even arrives. Some are depressed, feeling pressured by the past and propelled forward by feelings of guilt which goads them on to keep accomplishing.

The reality is that people with unbalanced or anomalous behavior often suffer from a mental illness. They're disconnected to the universal intelligence, God, and are out of balance. These are extreme conditions, and as such, they must be treated. Many people in our society live with this kind of "condition" every day. But there's always, always help.

Contemplating the past and the future will keep you stuck. Remember, most thoughts about the past or the future are false, exaggerated, and unrealistic.

The Time Is Now! You Have the Answer!
Write the first thought that came to mind and share one action step you will take to create the result you want.   **Date:** _____

_____

_____

_____

_____

Release The Emotional Mind and Ego Traps

All that we are is the result of what we have thought.
If a man speaks or acts with an evil thought, pain follows him.
If a man speaks or acts with a pure thought,
happiness follows him, like a shadow that never leaves him.

—Buddha

Secret 21 | Your mind is powerful.

Contemplation: Your mind creates either a negative or positive environment for you and the people around you. If you have any doubts about the power your mind has in influencing your reality, try this little experiment. Take a single thought and focus on it—just make up something and stay on it for a while—and tell me what happens after a few hours, or the next day, or next week. Your thought will become a reality.

Your mind has the ability to send your energy out into the world, and when it does so, it affects everyone and everything, even nature. This is why nature is "acting out" so ferociously these days; it's exactly the way the human mind is acting. There's no mystery to this: we are energy and we use it and we project it the same way as we possess it.

Attaining peace of mind in today's volatile world is of the utmost importance. I support anything you need to do to become peaceful. If you need medication, take it. If you are on a medical prescription, use it with balance. The simplest solution is to remember that your actions have far reaching consequences. Keep on constant watch. When you find yourself acting out, realize the damage you're inflicting on society as a whole. When you're stressed out, a thought you have or an action you take can be easily misinterpreted because of your stressed out condition.

In addition, think about the damage you're doing to your body's cells—they also get out of control, and when that cell breakdown occurs on the inside, the outside self reflects it. This is what causes you to age, to look older than you are, feel tired, and become sick.

Easier said than done? Get in touch with the child you once were, awaken to and remain aware of who you really are. You'll still go through life's obstacles and lessons, but you'll have a lot more fun living while you're learning!

The Time Is Now! You Have the Answer!
Write the first thought that came to mind and share one
action step you will take to create the result you want.   **Date:** _____

SECRET 22 | Your mind is a wanderer. It keeps traveling back through the past or into the future.

CONTEMPLATION: My friend Janine who was just about to start work as a photographer's assistant in New York City phoned me to talk about a dream she keeps having. She lives near the city, but in her dream she just can't seem to get to where she wants to go. She finds herself first in Akron, Ohio, where she grew up, and then, she's on a plane to New York, but instead finds herself in Paris, rollerskating with Barack Obama.

I'm not into Carl Jung's dream interpretations, but that one sounded almost like a parable to me. What we have for sure is the present moment, but instead we keep finding ourselves back in the Akron of the past—or else we shoot right pass the present and find ourselves in fantasyland, which is all the future can ever be. Doesn't that sound like a waste?

Humans have a tendency to want to take the easy road. They usually get stuck in the past, yet it's over. They keep doing things the same way to give themselves the illusion of doing something because this seems to bring a feeling of instant gratification and accomplishment. The future motivates them because it keeps people filled with hope. But now is when you can really succeed, just by being aware of the present moment.

I know you wonder, how do I do this? Well, stop reading for a moment. How eager are you to awaken to this present moment, to just be? Breathe in, consciously, and breathe out again—keep it up for ten minutes. Let the rest take its own course. Easy does it…

The Time Is Now! You Have the Answer!

Write the first thought that came to mind and share one action step you will take to create the result you want.   **Date:** _____

_____

_____

_____

_____

Secret 23 | Beware of your mind. Its nature is to play tricks on you.

Contemplation: Whatever you're struggling with right now, have you considered the two sides of the issue? Remember, the world we live in is bipolarized, but you don't have to be. Do not allow yourself to be judgmental about what's right or wrong. Living a balanced life is about (1) the choices you make, regardless of whether they are right or wrong, based on what's true for you; and (2) accepting that life can be right and wrong, and seeking the balance therein so you can stop driving yourself crazy.

Your mind, closely connected to your ego, is a trickster. On the other hand, the mind is your friend, and it protects you in times of danger by giving you a warning that you may be in danger. But in most cases, your mind is your biggest enemy.

For example, you know that something is good for you, such as eating healthy or exercising, but for some reason you just don't feel like it. You go to McDonald's instead and get yourself a double cheeseburger with fries, and then you return home and fall asleep. Your mind is keeping you from what's good for you.

Laziness is also a game of the mind, in my view. There are, of course, always exceptions to the rule. In life, your mind often keeps you from going where you want to go—it trips you up. Fear, doubts, insecurity, desperation, and low self esteem are all creations of the mind, not of the soul. They do not come from *The Source of Wealth in You*™.

The ego has a tendency to give you a false sense of being different than others. This is true on the outside, but deep within we're the same, connected in unity and spirit. The ego rules the outer (material) world. Your desires originate in the mind. In the spiritual world, however, the ego cannot do its tricks.

Living a truthful life and leading an authentic existence will require you to be able to recognize the Source from which your mind is operating so that when it's being a trickster, instead of a protector, you can catch it before it makes a mess in your life out of your purest, truest intentions!

As you know, I always advise you to seek the balance in any situation. Take the ego for what it is, and balance it against your soul—the true Source. Apply what I call THE SOURCE OF WEALTH IN YOU™ EGO PRINCIPLE©.

THE SOURCE OF WEALTH IN YOU™ EGO PRINCIPLE©

Consciously operate from *The Source of Wealth in You*™ (your soul and God residing within) by these practices:

- Practice constant awareness and control of your mind, ego, thoughts, actions, and reactions.
- Become practical.
- Take the best of both worlds (e.g., East/West; inner/outer), and only what works for you. Release what's useless to you.
- Take action!
- Always aim toward the middle; toward balance.

The ego is your biggest enemy most of the time. It will prevent you from becoming successful. I used to fall into that ego trap a great deal in my life. Today, I see the same happening to others each and every day!

For example, think of your mind as a nagging wife or husband always trying to control you. Control comes from insecurity. Your ego is so insecure that it can lead you to a complete disaster. There's nothing more dangerous than an insecure person. You never know what they're going to do because they do not own themselves and do not feel worthy of anything. Their ego is in total control.

Also, poor mind control leads to premature ejaculation (in men) or an inability to reach an orgasm (in women). A good example of perfect mind control is simultaneous orgasm, especially when each partner is able to release as soon as one informs the other. Remain constantly aware of your mind and the Source it operates from—distinguish it, balance it out, and you'll succeed.

Try this with me: Right now, your thoughts keep traveling in and out of your mind, and you have no peace within. Stop reading and start breathing properly again. When you return back to reading, this is what happened: Your breathing naturally slowed down after awhile and stopped. This is where the ultimate truth exists. Do not plan anything and release the expectations. Enjoy and witness your breath going in and out.

This is meditation. The greatest awakening for people occurs through proper breathing. Have fun with it every day. When you're faced with a decision, breathe instead of think. The answer will be revealed to you.

The Time Is Now! You Have the Answer!
Write the first thought that came to mind and share one
action step you will take to create the result you want.   **Date:** _____

_____

_____

_____

_____

SECRET 24 | One single thought can affect your whole day.

CONTEMPLATION: A thought that passes through your mind can become a reality within seconds.

This is exactly what happened to me one afternoon. Controlling my appetite is the hardest thing for me. So instead of keeping the whole bag of pistachios inside the house, where I'd be tempted to finish them off, I left it in my car trunk, so I would at least have to go to the garage to get some. Eventually, I went to my garage to get a handful of the pistachios I had bought the day before.

While I was at my car, a weird thought passed through my mind. I was looking at my chain with all the keys on it, and I thought, "I'd better remember to not close the trunk with the keys in it!" Within seconds, that's exactly what I did!

Without a key, I couldn't get back into my apartment unit, so I had to wait for someone to come out from one of the exits. When I got inside, I searched all over for an extra set of car keys, but I couldn't find it. I remembered that I had another set of keys locked in a little cabinet, and it took me an extra hour to break the lock—but no car keys were there. At last, I remembered where I had originally put the extra car keys, and I found them.

This whole ordeal had taken me almost three hours—and on a day when I had so much to do and already felt myself slipping behind! So then, of course, I started feeling stressed out about wasting all that time. I sat down hoping to unwind, and at last, after having lost almost half a workday, I went back to my work, rushing myself to catch up on it. I became really frustrated.

This is just one simple, real life example of what will happen when you're not aware of your thoughts. More than that, a thought leads to action. Can you now see how easy it is to turn your day into a mess? This is how it happens: (1) you are unaware of a thought that came into your mind; (2) you are not awake, and did not act fast enough to push that thought away before it turned into action, which caused chaos, as in the example above; and (3) you are not in control of your actions based on that thought.

Such events happen all the time, and this is how easy it is for our days to become unproductive. Whenever you hear someone say, "Well! This day really flew by! Where did the hours go?" it means one of two things:

(1) they were either so absorbed and wrapped up in what they love to do that time seemed to stop; or (2) they loused up the entire day with those hidden, negative thoughts that ended up wrecking and wasting their entire day!

This is why I keep talking about awareness. Your happiness really does depend on your level of awareness. Control of your thoughts and keeping the level of your awareness on high alert will determine the quality of your life.

The Time Is Now! You Have the Answer!

Write the first thought that came to mind and share one action step you will take to create the result you want.   ✒ DATE:_____

_____

_____

_____

_____

SECRET 25 | Caring for yourself, letting go, and controlling your mind will bring success into your life.

CONTEMPLATION: Life on Earth is temporary. We all know that, and it can make even the strongest person feel insecure deep inside, sometimes without even realizing it. For instance, when someone suddenly dies or life's unpleasant and sudden events leave you shaken, it really hits home; you awaken to the realization of how temporary our life on Earth is.

Our existence on Earth and in the physical body is brief. We're living our life here under certain conditions, and it may seem pointless. The point is that life on Earth is a test to pass and to pass it well. Remember, the real you is a soul, energy. Your body is young and healthy for a while, but when it starts getting older, taking care of it becomes difficult. On top of everything else we have to do in any given day—including work, family, shopping, entertaining ourselves and others—taking care of our body is a job by itself. It requires time and effort, such as clothing and exercising it to get rid of fat and toxins.

On top of it, fueling our body with good food is costly. But your soul needs a home—a body. This is why taking care of yourself both ways—inner and outer—must be a priority.

Humans want everything to last forever. But you know that will not happen; there isn't anything forever in this current lifetime. Our life on Earth is fleeting. You want to be in love forever, be happy forever, have plenty of excitement in life that lasts forever. But there's no such thing as "forever" here on Earth.

Life can definitely become complicated, and its dual nature often makes it appear even more so. Attachment to objects, people, or ways of living is very much part of human nature. It's difficult to let go. However, when you exist and operate from Source, you'll release the need for dependency, addictions, and unhealthy attachments. You'll rely on yourself exclusively.

You're taught what others believe is good for you. However, that is not always your truth. Only you can determine what is good and true for you. Others teach you what is good for them, or what they think is good for you. Listen to what they have to say, and if it feels good to you, try it to see if it works, and then move on to what really works for you.

Each time you catch yourself thinking, "I need to be right and to defend myself in this world," try switching the negative energy of this thought into a more empowering energy thought. Instead, take a breath and say to yourself: "I am one with others, in unity. I am here to give and to live in peace with others." It's amazing what a new attitude can do to create calm and peacefulness!

Here are a few suggestions to practice:

- Always try a different, more-effective approach to live your life. I know you want to make a difference in the world. I also know that you already are exceptional because you're God's creation. You want to reconnect to that incredible Source of pure energy within and get in touch with it. The question is: How strong and authentic is your desire to lead a successful, exceptional existence here on Earth? There might be some adjustments to make. However, it must be fun, and if it is not, do not do it.

- Discover a fun way of doing things. What does having fun look like to you? Remember, you are in control of your mind and ego. Controlling your mind, ego, and your thoughts will definitely bring more fun into your life. You must decide each day to either let your ego continue to play tricks on you and to let it take away the fun of living, or take the responsibility of controlling it by being consciously and constantly aware of its true nature.

Having control of your mind will lead to success, I promise. So, learning how to consciously become aware of what to let in and what to keep out will enable you to take control of your life. Choose what's good for you, not for everybody else.

The Time Is Now! You Have the Answer!
Write the first thought that came to mind and share one action step you will take to create the result you want.   DATE:_____

Secret 26 | Your mind says, "No" but your spirit says, "Yes, yes, yes!"

CONTEMPLATION: Become constantly aware of the fact that your mind might "think" that you do not deserve to be rich, happy, successful, or in love.

"No!" it whispers in your ear. "You think you can do that? Who do you think you're kidding?" It's the accumulation of all the negative energy you've ever absorbed and it knows how to knock you down.

I, personally, used to viscerally hate that voice because I didn't know how to take control of it, but once I became aware of it, I used to fight it viciously every single day. I still do. Now I know how to deal with it and that makes me feel good about myself. When I sometimes forget or when others come in with their egos snarling and yapping in front of me I literally get sick to my stomach.

Almost immediately after your birth, people started telling you "No." "Yes" and "no" are two of the first words you learned. And each time you heard the word "no," it translated to you as a barrier that would not allow any access to your power as an individual, to your Source of strength. You became confused and frustrated.

Today, you're away from those parental no's. Even if you still live at home, realize that "no" has very little power. Work patiently and calmly with your parents to lovingly show them that you have graduated into your own world, the world of "yes." Notice how you feel when you say that word out loud. "Yes, yes, yes! Yes, I am. Yes, I can. Yes, I deserve."

You're unique and you have the power and the potential to express your individuality. Become aware of and understand the conditioning that was imposed upon you as a child. It will remove the fear in your life. Most importantly, release the tendency to blame others. As I said before, there's no right or wrong, good or bad. It's how you choose to look at it. Make peace with the past, with your parents, society, and move on. You're given a certain period of time here on Earth to correct yourself, to transcend to a higher dimension and existence, so by all means, make the best of it!

You are free! How will you express your authentic self in the material world? This is your challenge, the reason for your creation, your life's mission. This is how you will create light and happiness.

The Time Is Now! You Have the Answer!
Write the first thought that came to mind and share one action step you will take to create the result you want.　　Date:_____

_____

_____

_____

_____

CREATE YOURSELF!

A journey of a thousand miles must begin with a single step.

—Lao-Tzu

Today is your day! Your mountain is waiting.
So…get on your way.

—Dr. Seuss

Secret 27 | I am who I am. But who and what am I?

CONTEMPLATION: The Greek philosopher and teacher Socrates said, "The unexamined life is not worth living." I love this quote!

Examining your life does not mean sifting through all your old baggage, revisiting over and over all the pain, regret, sorrow, and guilt of your past. It means examining your thoughts and actions with an eye to discover truths about yourself. It means seeking the answers and light within you. "What lies behind us and what lies before us," Emerson said, "are tiny matters compared to what lies within us." Isn't that wonderful? I also love this quote!

My life is exciting because I keep finding out more about myself every day; I never stop. I am extremely curious and can't stop myself from looking for more answers from within. The more I dig, the more I find, and it always leads me to more answers and brings me more happiness. If you don't feel comfortable with what you have found within, remember that you can always change the content. You're the artist, so you can do anything you want. The Source is in you. It's the permanent Source of Wealth.

The Time Is Now! You Have the Answer!
Write the first thought that came to mind and share one action step you will take to create the result you want.   DATE:_____

_____

_____

_____

_____

Secret 28 | How can I find out who I am and why I am here today?

CONTEMPLATION: Everyone wants to know the answer to "who am I and "why am I here?" This isn't something that originated with the psychedelic

'60s, I can assure you! Throughout antiquity, man has always wondered about this. Socrates was adamant about it when he said, "As for me, all I know is that I know nothing." And he was born in 469 BC!

So much for timeless wisdom! But truly, the answer lies within and always has. It's found through simplicity. I want to give you a piece of priceless life wisdom I've experimented with: When something feels uneasy, complicated, or awkward, it simply means that you might want to try a different way, a simpler way, or leave it alone for a while.

These days, everybody is looking for something higher than themselves as they take up yoga, meditation, and psychic and spiritual awareness classes. Recently, I was at my friend Laurence's birthday party, and he decided to do a meditation with me. When I saw the book he was using to practice the meditations, I couldn't even pronounce half the words and names I saw in it. It seemed really complicated. Certainly, many gurus out there use terms in Hindi and other languages. But why do we need to learn Hindi when we already have such difficulty just communicating in our own language? All we want is a simple answer. I can appreciate all forms on the way to self discovery and enlightenment, but honestly, I stay away from anything that feels like it will make my life complicated.

My point is, there are many different roads to the answers we seek. Most of us exclude the teachings that ask us to be satisfied with the sunshine and a little food and water. We're human, after all, and our nature is to constantly desire. Teachings like that will not work today in our material world. The truth is we want it all.

The solution I propose is to work out a balance between the ancient and the modern; it cannot be just one way. Nothing is ever one way; remember this and accept it. I've said it before, and I'll keep repeating it. *Use what you already have, what comes easy to you, what comes naturally, and this is your breath.* It's yours and you'll die without it—your breath. You can rediscover your real self simply through your own breath. THE SOURCE OF WEALTH IN YOU™ MEDITATION© will get you started and will help you to rediscover who you are and why you are here today. Any practice you undertake while using your breath is priceless. I use all of them however and whenever I want, and it's free! I don't even have to learn new terms and languages! Through breathing, you can reconnect and *Awaken to the Source of Wealth in You*™ anytime, anywhere.

The Time Is Now! You Have the Answer!
Write the first thought that came to mind and share one action step you will take to create the result you want.   🖋 DATE:_____

_____

_____

_____

_____

SECRET 29 | This lifetime is an opportunity to become one with yourself and God.

CONTEMPLATION: As soon as we come out of the womb we are immediately put through challenges. We begin the search for oneself and God; an ongoing search.

Why do you yearn for something greater? Because on a deeper level within, you feel a higher energy, a higher presence. You are searching for the energy of God that lives within and around you.

You came to Earth to express yourself fully and wholeheartedly. The search for oneself and God feels natural and authentic. You're constantly driven by your nature to learn more about yourself and others.

You have been given this life for a reason. You came here to reconnect, to create, to move toward the completion of one cycle to another. Or, you might have already gone through all cycles of birth and death. You might be on the way to the ultimate—a pure existence of eternal joy.

The only way to know God is by knowing yourself because God and you are one. This is the only chance you have, right now, in this lifetime. Right now, accept yourself and God as one. Realize that your current life is your mission to get closer to yourself and God.

The Time Is Now! You Have the Answer!
Write the first thought that came to mind and share one action step you will take to create the result you want.　　🌿Date: _____

_____

_____

_____

_____

Secret 30 | You came on Earth to create your life just as God created you.

CONTEMPLATION: When you awaken to the fact that you have a special purpose in this lifetime, you'll automatically become the creator of your life. Do you believe in the interconnectedness of it all? You've witnessed how one thing leads to another. Taking into consideration that life on Earth is temporary, and you are merely an actor who plays a role here ("all the world's a stage," Shakespeare so aptly reminded us), then you'll see that there's no way you can keep yourself from creating; each one of you is a creator of your own life.

You might ask the question, what about God? God created you so that you too may create and procreate in unison with God.

What happens when you feel stuck in your life, when it feels like nothing is happening? It means that you've stopped creating. When you stop, everything stops. You are here to create in order to live. Only then your true gift, skill, talent, mission, and purpose will reveal itself. But you have to start, to initiate and take action—and on the way, you'll find out what works and what doesn't. Take a tiny step today!

Attaining knowledge, along with action, is a prerequisite for creating a new, meaningful life of joy and happiness. In addition, it's important for you to develop good imagination. Each one of you has it. Think about those dirty little secrets that you hold inside that no one knows about.

Here's how it works: My friend Steve always imagined himself as a matador when he was a little boy. Today, his sexual fantasy is an encounter with a female matador. I notice how he even runs his life like a matador, getting involved with powerful women just like the female matador he likes to imagine. Here again is a great example of the connectedness of it all in action. Recall your childhood fantasies and those of the present to create your life today—and your tomorrows.

If you believe, as I do, that the physical world we live in is a dream, you can start creating like mad. I, personally, am a master of abundant, wild, vivid imagination. I have to tell you, everything I have imagined has become true and real for me. This is why I am not motivated by fear. When I imagine something, I'm so certain about it that I live it daily as if it has already happened. Trust me on this one—all you need is to awaken your ability to imagine, create, and take action on it. It happens to me every day—my imaginations turn into reality. I promote and teach wild, fearless imagination combined with action as the road to success and happiness.

The Time Is Now! You Have the Answer!
Write the first thought that came to mind and share one action step you will take to create the result you want.   DATE:_____

SECRET 31 | We come from perfection. Our life's purpose is to reconnect with it.

CONTEMPLATION: Some people work very hard. The secret to life, however, is to not work hard at all, but to exist peacefully. The key is to reach a point where you can just "be" and enjoy life's abundance without looking for it. What you attract will be exactly what you need and the way it's supposed to be. What I'm talking about is possible and real, and not hard to reach.

Returning to perfection is to simply awaken—to become conscious, wake up and to open your eyes, to know a truth from a lie, and to experience rebirth, renewal, and revival. If you feel tired all the time, it's no wonder—you have not yet awakened to the universe, God, and to your true self! You're kind of numb inside and out, or maybe even sick.

You took the first step toward awakening when you left your mother's womb: you took a breath. You bawled; you screamed. You were then breathing fully, wholesomely. Then you started growing up and the older you got, the shallower your breathing became. You were afraid to let a breath out.

Why does this happen? Because in the physical world in which we live we are told what to do from the minute we begin to conceptualize the meanings of words. "Be quiet when Mommy's sleeping"; "Don't play so loud"; and "No screaming in the car!" After three or so years of hearing this (or more, depending on your level of natural exuberance), we are pressured to mute ourselves.

Most people only breathe halfway, barely at all. How often do you consciously witness the air going in and out of your nostrils and feel your diaphragm moving in and out along with it? Probably never, and that's one of the reasons why you're not quite awake! Learn to breathe and be completely conscious of your breathing. I call the body "a breathing machine." When you start running it properly, you'll awaken.

Learn how to breathe and watch what happens: synchronicities, orderliness, joy, and happiness will start to appear in your life. It's the most important breath you'll ever take because it leads to perfection.

The Time Is Now! You Have the Answer!
Write the first thought that came to mind and share one
action step you will take to create the result you want. 🖋Date:_____

_____

_____

_____

_____

Secret 32 | If you want an answer and you're confused about your life, keep searching within. The only true answer can be found in you.

Contemplation: When you become restless at work, at home, or you can't sleep at night, you're experiencing the outward signs of inner struggle. Thinking over and over can drag you into the past or push you into the future; it can torture you with memories or tempt you with fantasies that may not happen.

When you need an answer to a question, follow these steps:

1. Remain here, in this moment.
2. Set aside fifteen minutes a day for yourself to just practice proper breathing—The Source of Wealth in You™ Meditation©—so you can get used to it and exist from it all the time. If you don't like sitting, you can practice it walking or dancing, but breathe consciously. Do what suits you and feels good to you.
3. See the answer revealed to you already. If you're unable to do so—imagine it.
4. How does it feel?
5. Feel it!
6. Then, let it go!

Through meditation and application of the 117 Secrets and powerful exercises in this book, you will begin to experience wonders. For example, when I've planned to do something and in the meantime, before I even get to it, I realize that I have already done it! Or, if I happen to think about someone, just the passing thought of that person will naturally attract their energy into my life and the events will follow. In other words, I discover that a natural resolution and synchronicities in my dealings with that person have taken place: they have received a message from me, the universe, and from God. This is unity—we're one.

Our thoughts turn into actions and realizations. When you're connected to God, you don't need to do much. The most exciting part on the journey of life is when you naturally draw from the Source without thinking about it. Then life becomes easier. You meld with the flow of life. Confusion, procrastination, and doubt will not exist. This is what I call being alive, living a life of truth. Can life get more exciting than that? It's a relief, trust me!

The Time Is Now! You Have the Answer!
Write the first thought that came to mind and share one action step you will take to create the result you want.   **Date:** _____

_____

_____

_____

_____

_____

Secret 33 | One of the greatest reasons we came here is to discover, to express a unique gift and to use it for the goodness of all.

CONTEMPLATION: Each one of you has many gifts, but there's a unique gift, a special talent that only you can share. It's an extraordinary gift.

But how aware are you of the special gift you're blessed with? How are you making use of it? I know it's easier sometimes to just ignore it. You can remain in your comfort zone or think of yourself as a victim of life's circumstances, and odd as it may sound, that indeed can feel perversely comforting. But it will come back to get you. This is what the PRINCIPLE OF CAUSE AND EFFECT©, aka Karma, is about. There are no free or easy rides on the journey of life on Earth. You came here to earn it for yourself. If you don't, you will suffer.

Human beings are creatures of comfort and that is exactly what's being offered out there, everywhere in the world of our senses. Just look around and you'll see. This is why so many people are stuck with low self esteem, feeling insecure, or handicapped for life. This is how life on Earth is structured, so you can pick yourself up, awaken, and express who you really are—rediscover, awaken, and operate from *The Source of Wealth in You*™.

I believe that God challenges us. Our parents challenge and coax us to talk and walk, much the same way that God stands back and watches us when we're going through a particularly difficult time. God wants to see what we're made of, so to speak. And we have to prove it not only to God, but to ourselves—because we are connected to God and God is love and because we are love as well!

The fact is that no one will live your life for you or discover and express your gift for you. You can draw strength and guidance from different resources, but you have to put in some effort to work on yourself a bit.

We came here to improve the conditions of the world and to make it more beautiful, a better place. Becoming a true contributor in your own life, in the lives of others, and to society as a whole makes you a leader. The only difference between your leadership and others' is the foundation it operates from. Today, rebuild and begin to exist from a new solid inner (spiritual) foundation that carries over its strength to the outer (physical, material) world. When you do that, a new life direction and the answers will be naturally revealed to you.

Anything coming from your authentic self is lasting and meaningful because it comes from pure honesty.

The Time Is Now! You Have the Answer!
Write the first thought that came to mind and share one action step you will take to create the result you want.   **Date:** _____

Secret 34 | Just like your fingerprints, your gift is uniquely yours. Expressing it is your life's mission, purpose and way to happiness.

Contemplation: Your gift, as unique as your fingerprints, is to be expressed and shared with others. Once you reveal it to yourself and to others, wealth and success will follow you.

In countries like the United States, a person's sense of worth usually depends on his/her material accomplishments—what they do, how much money they make, what they own, and so forth. This is how one's occupation, or vocation, becomes their very identity. Yet deep inside, the person who seems to have it all is often unhappy, taking medications to numb the pain, or keeping a family together for the sake of money and society's principles.

Why is it this way? Because people don't make themselves a priority—to relax and take time to address whatever must be addressed, resolved, and taken care of. When you devote time to yourself, success in the different areas of your life will naturally take its own course. You will become more aware of what to do and how to do it because you will feel worthy enough to invest the time in yourself.

Most people feel a sense of worth when they're acknowledged for what they have to offer. A great way to live a successful life is to ask yourself this question each day: What can I offer, to give of myself today, so I can improve my life and the lives of others? When you make it a habit to ask yourself this question every morning, and look into your soul in a selfless way as you answer it, you will feel a sense of greater purpose and meaning added to your daily life. I do not promote receiving without giving and the giving always comes first.

Life is a vicious circle, and it is easy for humans to go right along with it, repeating the same mistakes over and over. This is how people many end up spending their whole life. The more time you invest in yourself, the more you will be able to bring out of yourself and give to the world—which is what you came here for, isn't it?

The only way to make this happen is to invest a little time each day into discovering your true gift through the core of your being. It's like a daily workout routine: if you work out every day, you will look great. Then, when you see the outcome from it, it becomes addictive. The hardest part is getting started—being devoted, disciplined, and making yourself a priority. It's called giving—to yourself and to others.

The Time Is Now! You Have the Answer!
Write the first thought that came to mind and share one action step you will take to create the result you want.   **Date:** _____

_____

_____

_____

_____

SECRET 35 | We came into this world to transform our negative nature into positive.

CONTEMPLATION: Life can be complicated. Why is that? Why isn't there only joy and happiness? What is happening when everything seems to fall down upon you? You're being divinely challenged!

Stop to reconsider your life and the adjustments you need to make so you can rise above your own self and adversity. In the material world we live in, negativity breeds upon itself. There's far too much negativity in the world—just look around, and you'll see plenty of it.

Make sure you're the first to take action to eliminate negativity from your life. You may ask, Why do I have to be the first one to take action? Why not let the other person go first? Here's the ego talking to your insecure mind. Each person's mind works the same way. You must initiate action. By being the first one to do so, you're reclaiming your individuality. If you find that you can't, it may be that you're confined in the boundaries of the material world and cannot see the bigger picture on a spiritual level.

Simply initiate a change in yourself. Others are just as insecure as you are and maybe even more so. Awareness and regaining control of your mind and ego will help you overcome your selfish nature. Then, you'll be in a position to make a difference in the lives of others who are struggling just like you.

My friends range from teenagers to people close to one hundred years old. I see many lost souls of all ages. Of course, a few years ago, I was a lost soul myself. I was completely lost and had no idea what to do with my life. I found that working with my selfish nature continuously—I really mean that, nonstop—led me to reconnect with the true me: my soul and God.

To initiate a change, follow these steps:

- Be the first one to initiate a resolution by taking action. Respond with the true, authentic, happy side of you.

- Counteract the existing negativity with the opposite—the positive—to create love, light, joy, and happiness.

- Recognize that your ego is trying to prevent you from following through on your goals. This is its nature—to play games with your soul.
- Remain detached from the ego trap of other human beings.
- Consciously use your natural born leadership qualities.
- Always operate from *The Source of Wealth in You*™—the pure Source within, and God.

The Time Is Now! You Have the Answer!
Write the first thought that came to mind and share one action step you will take to create the result you want. **Date:** _____

Secret 36 | You're exceptional, accept it!

Contemplation: Most of us have been pressured to "fit in" from our earliest days. But how can you fit in when you don't yet know who you are and what your purpose is in this lifetime? It's impossible—so it's no wonder most people are unhappy!

You haven't been encouraged to express yourself as exceptional, but you are. You have not been or ever will be ordinary. You, me, and all humans and living things—we are exceptional. We have a purpose, a mission to live by.

To discover how amazing you are, know yourself. It's an internal journey—one you may undertake alone or with the assistance of someone to oversee the steps you're taking (not a shoulder to cry on). There are some qualified individuals qualified, such as an awakened life coach or an enlightened spiritual teacher. They will guide you toward happiness, success, joy, and transcendence by assisting you to reconnect to your authentic self. If you feel you really need this kind of support in your life, visualize this type of person coming into your life. See it happening as you breathe in and out. As with anything, if you focus on it and you're filled with certainty, you will attract this person into your life.

We've been influenced by all kinds of influences since we were conceived. Remember, the physical self is temporary. Your inner self is pure. It's energy. It just is. It is God within you. The connection between your physical self and your spiritual self is essential and not just for some of the time, but always. When it happens, it releases suffering. I now ask you to consider the following:

- Right now, you might be confused and a divided being. You're this way because you live in the material world—a dual world. This is why you're in emotional pain. I am proposing a solution, an antidote—that you become whole again. After all, what is more valuable than to reconnect your body, mind, and soul?

- What is more important to you than to exist naturally, with ease, and become in tune with our perfect universe? Consciously align your own existence with perfection. Practice until it reveals itself to you. Meditate.

- How long are going to suffer and allow the energy to be drained out of you? It's up to you. Meditate.

Acknowledge that you already are exceptional. Get in touch with the exceptional in you and give the same. Then, you will respectfully receive the same. Ask yourself this question and answer it below: How willing and open are you to accept the fact, once and forever, that you deserve the best, and you don't have to suffer for it? The following is what matters:

- Right now, accept that you are exceptional. Believe it with certainty and notice how life becomes easier for you.

- Stay in this moment, also known as "the now," and breathe consciously. Make conscious breathing part of your daily life, just like brushing your teeth after each meal. Start to notice how the future will begin to take care of itself automatically.

The only way you can discover anything is by practice and experimentation. Reading alone will not do it. So, start with me today. Keep in mind, the way things happen and work for you will not be the way they work for anyone else because there's no one else like you. You're exceptional and always will be! Accept the exceptional!

The Time Is Now! You Have the Answer!
Write the first thought that came to mind and share one action step you will take to create the result you want.   **Date:**_____

_____

_____

_____

_____

Secret 37 | In fact, you're a genius!

Contemplation: I'm convinced that there's a true genius in each one of us. However, there's a fine line between you, the genius, and your ego. The challenge arises when you cannot separate your ego from your innate, natural exceptional abilities. The two can become entangled.

A true genius leads a life where the ego is kept under control. It does not interfere with what he or she already has—a natural Source of divine potential—*The Source of Wealth in You*™.

I love psychology, but to tell you the truth, some people have been going to counseling and therapy most of their life and not a lot has changed for them. I myself have tried counseling. I was so desperate a few years ago I'd try anything. So I went to several different psychologists to see if I could find "the right one," but I felt none were "right" for me. I couldn't make myself stay with any of them for more than a few sessions.

I stopped searching for my elusive happiness that way, but I still ask myself why people keep going to their weekly sessions. I now have the answer, but it took me some time to figure it out.

Even caregivers need care themselves. Quite often, there is no one to give the true genius the support he or she needs too. Some of them go and have a weekly talk with a psychologist—a shrink. In fact, one of my exceptional friends is Dr. Steiner. A true genius at what he does, he's devoted himself to the lives of others. He really doesn't care how he looks, where he lives, or what kind of car he drives. He only cares about others' health and well being. He sometimes even overlooks his own health to devote time to others.

Dr. Steiner still feels guilty about his broken marriage that ended in divorce because he gave so much of himself to others and consequently had little time left for his spouse. But he is the best father imaginable to his two wonderful sons.

And here's another insight: Dr. Steiner has been in therapy all of his life. Haven't you heard the saying, "A surgeon can't operate on himself"? I think Dr. Steiner is still in therapy because he's being supported on the basic societal level of well being, but he's a genius. He also has not yet learned to receive, to strike that balance between giving and receiving, because he spends all day, nearly every day, giving so much of himself.

A genius needs more than the ordinary; more than basic care. This is you I'm talking about! Each one of you is exceptional! On a deeper level, you know you deserve the best. This is why you keep searching for happiness and why many of you keep going to a psychologist.

Therapy didn't work for me and may not work for many people. That's why we're all so delightfully different; our needs vary, even as we move through the seasons of our lives. Sometimes we feel we need to conform and other times we don't. The most important rule is that you're an individual.

I am blessed to have discovered the Source of happiness—myself—my inner Source. Patiently revisit your own inner Source to rediscover and to unveil the wealth, so you can get in touch with the genius within and will learn how to rely on yourself.

The Time Is Now! You Have the Answer!
Write the first thought that came to mind and share one action step you will take to create the result you want.   ❧Date:_____

_____

_____

_____

_____

Secret 38 | There's always an exception to the rule and you're it!

Contemplation: A lot of my friends are high achievers and smart, successful individuals.

They have discovered their life's mission. I am sure it wasn't easy. It wasn't easy for me. I'm glad I went through the experiences to have arrived where I am today. Today, I'm certain my life is meaningful, not only to me, but it's tailored to improve the lives of millions of people around the world, and help them to experience rebirth, transformation, joy, and happiness.

Even the most successful, materially wealthy individuals live with doubt, fear, and insecurities—all the time. On the inside we are the same, all God's creatures. On the outside we are different from each other, still God's creatures. So where does the truth lie? In the middle, in God's unity. We cannot see God with our eyes but deep within "we know" God exists, just like we're certain we love our children and the animals in our lives.

I have always been impressed by a man I'll call Ben who has done wonders for humanity. I was thinking of getting in touch with him to partner up because I know two heads are better than one and I personally enjoy teamwork.

When I got in touch with Ben, we clicked right away. After a few conversations, he trusted me enough to let me know what was going on in his life. Interestingly, I had caught Ben at a phase when he was going through some "bad times." I applied my skills to find out what was really going on. He was feeling down, like everyone, because of the economic crisis. He wasn't sure if he could raise enough money to complete a project he had already started. He said that "his people" were not sure if they were going to invest in his project—or any other projects at the time. While he was going through turmoil, feeling down and insecure about his future success, I was able to help him understand that his future is in his own hands.

First, I told him that by having doubts he'd attract doubts and his investors would pick up on his energy and would start doubting the success of this project, period. Remember, we are connected through energy.

Second, I told him that what is currently down must come up, and times will get better because it's inevitable. Where else is his life going if not up, when down? This is simple quantum physics; life is pure energy which is about movement and change. Change is inevitable.

Third, I asked him if he had accepted this very important rule in life: that "there's always an exception to the rule"—and why wouldn't he be the exception this time? This kind of crisis had happened to him before and he had enjoyed great success. Even if he had not achieved success before, why wouldn't it happen to him this one time?

He immediately recognized the authenticity of my comments. I knew that when Benjamin accepted the fact that he is an exception to the rule, the type of energy he exuded would reach a similar type of energy channel and it would be felt by others.

I see it every day—people lose everything, and they clam up again. This is life—a constant flux. Remember this and accept the fact that whatever is happening to you right now will not remain the same. By shifting your own energy, you'll become the cause, the effect, and an exception to the rule.

Try shifting your energy and see what happens. By working with me, here in this book, you're now learning how to recover from the daily negativity you encounter in the material world. The tools are right in front of you; use them!

The Time Is Now! You Have the Answer!

Write the first thought that came to mind and share one action step you will take to create the result you want.   ❦ Date:_____

_____

_____

_____

_____

Secret 39 | Aim daily toward balance! Trust yourself!

CONTEMPLATION: Most people keep going around in circles looking for answers. Your answers are usually affected by the information you receive from outside sources. There is so much of it, coming from different religions, philosophies, the news you see on TV or read in the paper and the information you're exposed to on the Internet every day. It's enough to make the fastest multi-tasker's head spin. To live a harmonious life, begin to apply daily what I call the BALANCING ACT PRINCIPLE©.

BALANCING ACT PRINCIPLE©

Bring in the two opposites—"the outer" *against* "the inner"—together by balancing:

- what you're presented with from the world you reside in (that is, what you hear "out there," which is usually negative) against

- what is true for you (which, when coming from your soul, is positive).

When you consciously bring in the two opposites together toward the middle, balance and happiness will appear. Practice this principle in any life situation you're presented with.

People don't trust themselves. When your inner voice—your intuition—speaks, recognize it. You believe in God and in the universe, but you don't believe in yourself! If you tune in and listen to the messages that come your way and you keep yourself alert for them, they will manifest in your life. They are there for you, always available.

For example, I was on my treadmill at home one day, "thinking" about an issue that was troubling me, while watching TV at the same time. I wasn't really paying much attention to the TV, but suddenly—boom! There it was—a guy on a soap opera as I was flipping through the channels said something that was so right, so meant for me that it made me shiver; it felt like a wave of complete recognition went through my body. I knew this was the answer to a question I had been asking myself for a while. This is exactly how you receive the answers you are looking for—they can come through an outside source. Tune in to hear them.

The truth is revealed through you and to you. The outside sources will serve you well if you are tuned in, not just by listening to the information and what others are telling you, but by being open to the messages behind it. Listen, and feel it in your body. If you get goose bumps, you know it's true. This is what it means to be centered, balanced, and in the middle. You have the answers within.

You come from truth. Reach for it by trusting your intuition and the universal messages. Balance the two sides—the two extremes, the inner with the outer, the positive with the negative, the black with the white—toward the middle, toward balance. This is your challenge for this lifetime, and you are here to meet it! Rediscover the pure you and your mission—now, as opposed to continuing to live a life of illusion. What's waiting for you next? It depends on the seeds you sow right here, right now, today!

The Time Is Now! You Have the Answer!

Write the first thought that came to mind and share one action step you will take to create the result you want.   **Date:** _____

Everything Is Energy

We are all spiritual beings having a human experience.

—Pierre Teilhard de Chardin

Secret 40 | There are no coincidences. All has meaning.

Contemplation: I find a reason, a message, in every encounter and every thought that travels through my mind. It's the same with my actions. It's as simple as going to the bathroom. What is the reason we go? We know it means our body needs to release certain toxins that have accumulated. There is a reason, a purpose, behind everything we do.

Experiment with this, and you'll find meaning in everything; you'll start to awaken to your life's truths. Keep asking the questions, write down the answers, and witness how life becomes fun.

At first, it may seem difficult to catch each fleeting thought. The more you awaken inwardly and start to consciously exist, you'll begin to notice each thought; it will become second nature to you. In most cases, every thought you have is connected to what's happening in your life on a subconscious level. The subconscious is where the truth and Source reside. You may be picking on someone's energy, or perhaps you're thinking about a particular issue a great deal. I have experimented with this a lot just to convince myself. Can you now see how living life fully is fun, like a game? It's meant to be!

There's a plus side, a lesson to be learned, in any negativity, just as there's always a minus side to all the greatest pluses in your life. I always check both—the pluses and the minuses—and balance them out.

There's no such thing as good or bad, per se. The mind is a control freak, trying to dominate your spiritual energy. That's why being in tune with yourself and the universal energy, God, can toss out negative thoughts and help you remain true to your authentic self.

But back to coincidences. You did not come here by accident. I know there's a whole story behind your creation. Have you ever tried to look at that story? Have you tried writing it down? The story we carry inside us is one reason that we all have such need to express ourselves. You want to share this greatness! Writing is a wonderful way to express your inner self, to release what may be holding you back.

You are supposed to be here in this form and shape at this particular time. Where you are in your life right now is exactly where you're supposed to be, no question about it. Accept it, release what's holding you back, meditate, love, and work with yourself. Breathe! It's all you can do, and it's all you're meant to do.

The Time Is Now! You Have the Answer!
Write the first thought that came to mind and share one
action step you will take to create the result you want.   🌿 Date: _____

_____

_____

_____

_____

Secret 41 | The universe sends perfect messages. Can you hear them?

CONTEMPLATION: When something in your life may seem to have gone wrong or the opposite of what you've planned, it's probably for your own good. Haven't you ever experienced a time when you wanted something bad enough only to have the opposite happen but it's left you with a great sense of relief?

Here's how a simple incident can reveal a resolution. Let's say you were looking forward to getting together with your friend, but he/she cancels the original plan or changes it because of some problems in his/her own life he/she has to deal with or because something came up. Most of the time, there's a good reason for the cancellation or setback, although it may not seem that way to you on the surface. There might also be something you need to resolve in your own life.

For example, I was looking forward to having a fun evening with a man I was dating I'll call Adam. We decided to make it a special night and not talk about work but to just have fun watching movies all night and to enjoy a warm, intimate evening. I wanted him to stay with me all night. So we planned that for Monday night. As the day progressed, I began to feel a bit stressed out, overwhelmed, and uneasy.

Later, he called to tell me that we could get together for a little bit, but he won't be able to stay long because he had something important to deal with early next morning. "Let's just forget the whole thing," I said. "Well, it's up to you," he responded. When I got off the phone I felt hurt and angry. At first, I had an ache inside—the sort of lover's ache that makes you feel as though you've got poison circulating in your veins. But fortunately, I recognized the falseness of that feeling and knew how to get past it.

I went for a walk in the park while listening to a self help audio. Suddenly, something I heard on the audio gave me the answer to a relationship issue I'd been dealing with for some time. And it came to me precisely because Adam had given me the solitude I needed to hear that message from the universe. There were signals for me to pay attention to and to not get upset at him, but it took me a few hours to get over it. See, it wasn't about the other person it was about me.

When you are in control of your ego, your mind, and your emotions, you will hear the messages. The universal intelligence, God, is always working in your interest. There is a perfect order out there, so stay tuned.

The Time Is Now! You Have the Answer!
Write the first thought that came to mind and share one action step you will take to create the result you want.   DATE:_____

SECRET 42 | Thoughts and actions have consequences.

CONTEMPLATION: Iconic singer songwriter John Lennon wrote about "Instant Karma," but sometimes it may take a little longer. Whatever you do to another living or nonliving thing is what you get in return—if not now, definitely later, guaranteed.

In my own life, I have awakened to this universal Law of Cause and Effect, aka Karma. I now practice positive thinking, patience, and restriction because I know that the kind of thoughts, words, actions, and reactions I have will encounter the same.

Let me show you how Karma works indirectly in our lives; how what you do returns to you in the same exact way. For example, we do lots of business through email—you send an email and you receive a reply. The other person is waiting to hear from you again but you spend some time doing other things, waiting for some time to pass.

You want to send your reply and to get the other person's answer right then, but you also want to show how busy you are—even if you're not that busy at all! When you finally write back, you wait impatiently, but the other person takes awhile to respond too—also playing the same sort of ego game without even realizing it. The "waiting game" is another example of the ego's need to express itself. Can you see how this whole mind ego game starts and then turns into Karma?

What you do will be done to you in the same exact way. What you give will be given to you too. The same is true for all the beautiful things in life. When you do, give and say something nice to someone, you will receive the same in return. In addition, by doing so you're opening the door to a positive energy flow exchange—letting the good energy flow out, thus allowing it to come back.

Try it today. Smile at a total stranger and notice how long it takes before he/she smiles back at you. Acknowledge how much happier you feel!

The Time Is Now! You Have the Answer!

Write the first thought that came to mind and share one action step you will take to create the result you want.   **Date:** _____

_____

_____

_____

_____

Secret 43 | The Principle of Cause and Effect© is inescapable. Time may be the only delay.

Contemplation: This is one of the few guarantees in life: Whatever is happening, there is always a reason for it, a cause. There's also an effect of that cause. You probably already know that from basic science or history classes, or from just living.

Today, I remain constantly aware of the Principle of Cause and Effect©. If by chance I missed it, then when the consequence hits me, I know exactly what I did. But why wait until you get hit? There are so many things that have happened in between the cause and the effect that you could have readjusted earlier to prevent an unwanted consequence—a terrible loss or whatever it might be.

When it comes to the Principle of Cause and Effect©, you're the only one who controls it. You're in total charge of it and cannot run away from it. It's another law of physics: you simply cannot escape the consequences of your thoughts, actions, reactions, etc. Not one single time have I been able to escape from it, and there was a period of my life when I was always running away, including running away from myself.

But what does that mean? It means that my mind took complete possession of my whole being. I wasn't in control of myself, my thoughts or my actions, therefore I had to face the consequences. Then I stopped. I couldn't run away from life; the running had become too exhausting, and I felt drained, and then I crashed. But I learned one thing: I needed to face life head on. It can be scary, but if you don't, life will chase you right into the grave.

Become aware of the PRINCIPLE OF CAUSE AND EFFECT©. Make a choice today to remain aware of your thoughts, actions, and reactions to prevent yourself from unwanted consequences. Certainly, you may have many negative thoughts, but check to see how authentic they are and on what they are based:

1. Always look at the Source—where the thought is coming from—is it fear? anger? denial? or a feeling of unworthiness?

2. Determine if the thought is yours or if it comes from an outside source, someone else, etc. Check that out and immediately look into your real source (your soul), and God (the Source) too—*The Source of Wealth in You*™.

Keep in mind that you can only be temporarily misled—ultimately you know the truth.

The Time Is Now! You Have the Answer!
Write the first thought that came to mind and share one action step you will take to create the result you want.   ♪DATE:_____

SECRET 44 | You create your life with each thought.

CONTEMPLATION: Thoughts are like magnets. A thought comes in and soon enough the actualization of it appears. Your thoughts determine the outcome of your life. Your success and happiness depend on the following two things:

- **BEING AWAKE.** You meditate and practice proper breathing daily as a regular workout routine for the mind, so you can control your thoughts.
- **BEING VIGILANT.** Your ability to quickly recognize when a single thought comes in. You can choose to keep it or refuse to accept it. This is the way to fully take control of your life. Thoughts become realizations: thoughts become "things."

Train yourself to see the positive side of even an extremely complicated, negative situation. There's always a positive side to even the worst scenario. Remember, when you develop a habit to focus on, the positive you will exude and attract back to you a flow of the same energy. That alone will accelerate a positive resolution of the issue you're dealing with.

How can you separate your thoughts like that? How can you latch onto the positive ones and discard the negative ones when you have so many of them coming at you, one after another, almost at the same time, and your head is spinning?

You must control your thoughts. Clear some space in your life to reconnect to the peace and tranquility already available within. Meditation brings self-awareness which is the best way to control your thoughts, to heal, to become love, and to remain happy.

When something is good for you but it feels like you don't want to do it, or it can even feel like torture, do you know what that means? It means that your mind wants control over you. Calmly thank your mind for trying to "protect you" from what is good for you and do it anyway.

You create your life through your thoughts that turn into actions. Today you can begin to create a better life for yourself and others by sifting through your thoughts. Quickly discard the thoughts that are poisonous because the ones you accept will become your reality.

The Time Is Now! You Have the Answer!

Write the first thought that came to mind and share one
action step you will take to create the result you want. **Date:** _____

Secret 45 | You are life; you are energy. It's about you.

Contemplation: Rebuilding your inner (spiritual) foundation will determine the events on the outside (the material world). It stems from you—the way you are and the way you want to be. I know that this book will help you understand how important you are and how the whole world depends on you because you're an essential part of it. The fact that you're here today is the best thing that happened to this world. It is your duty to fulfill an obligation to yourself and to others by honoring your creation, your Creator, life, and existence.

We came here to experience bliss in a world of beauty and chaos. What a challenge! We came on Earth to give. I promote riches, material and spiritual, inner and outer. Each one of us deserves riches. Once you realize that you are abundance, riches will find you. You are not a victim. You do not have to be a victim of life's circumstances; not ever.

On the journey of life, there's only enlightenment to be found. Rebuild your own strong foundation and transform your character and behavior so you can assist others as well. Isn't it worth it to prepare yourself for others? You're the most important creature, energy force, spirit, walking body, anything you want to call yourself. You are the ultimate. You are life! It starts with you!

The Time Is Now! You Have the Answer!

Write the first thought that came to mind and share one action step you will take to create the result you want. **Date:**_____

_____

_____

_____

_____

Secret 46 | The human energy field is tied to its surroundings. The perfect connection between the two represents inner peace and happiness.

Contemplation: I have been focusing on "you" as the navigator of your life. However, you cannot work in isolation but only in connection with the universe, God. How do you connect the material world with the unseen world of God?

As we know, energy, God, is everywhere. We cannot exist without it, as we cannot exist without the light of the sun. To experience the connection between you and the invisible forces operating on a higher frequency, consciously align your inner self with your physical environment.

To give you a simple example, let's focus on your home. Your home is a special place to retreat, rejuvenate, contemplate, and to connect with yourself and God. It's a place that helps you avoid operating from a state of confusion. Consider the following:

♦ How does your home feel when you walk inside after a busy day at work? Are you still stressed out or does it feel good to be home? Is everything as you would like it to be?

- Does the way things are situated inside give you a sense of peace and calm, or do you feel like you have to start all over again, to work hard to straighten it out?

When people come to my home, many of them claim to feel more peaceful, positive, and enlightened. Why do they feel this way? It's because I spend time rearranging my home to honor the energy flow in there.

Follow your inner guidance, intuition, your gut, and notice when something feels off. Figure out what it is, and act on it without procrastination. Invest some time to align your surroundings with the perfect flow of the universal energy and more time will be available to you to do what's important and good for you. I call this true, authentic living. This is the road to happiness.

The Time Is Now! You Have the Answer!
Write the first thought that came to mind and share one action step you will take to create the result you want. ❤ DATE:

SECRET 47 | Your energy mirrors all you encounter.

CONTEMPLATION: Who and what you are at this particular time and place is exactly who and what you will attract. If you don't like it, become a different character in your movie called "Life."

Have you noticed that when your life is kind of a mess, more chaos keeps coming into your life? Then it becomes unbearable. It keeps on coming; it does not end. Where does it come from? It comes from you. I have devoted lots of time to experimenting with this truth. It always comes from you.

You're the Source of it because you're made of energy and surrounded by it. Energy attracts energy.

Become who and what you want in your life. The rest will show up.

The Time Is Now! You Have the Answer!
Write the first thought that came to mind and share one action step you will take to create the result you want.   ❥Date:_____

_____

_____

_____

_____

Secret 48 | Your energy affects the whole universe.

CONTEMPLATION: Energy is everywhere, all around us. We're made from it and surrounded by it. The universe is charged with energy and its constant signals and messages. Information travels through energy channels. Life, God, you—all of this is energy, all connected. When you've awakened, you can feel the energy—your own, other people's, and the universe's—and you can take control of your life. Even if you are not exactly sure of what's going on inside of you, others can pick up on your energy, thoughts, and feelings—sometimes better than you can!

The channels through which energy transmits are like satellites; they circle around you, and they pick up everything. You can keep denying something to yourself, but others can sense your energy. Your emotions and feelings affect others: when you're angry or anxious your energy reaches them. Here's my energy principle of how the universe works: I call this the PRINCIPLE OF TRANSFERABLE ENERGY©.

Principle of Transferable Energy©

The thoughts someone has for you will reach you from far away. It will affect your whole being just as if they had physically touched you or spoken to you. Now, remember, you can actually get sick from negative thoughts—yours and others.' Their thoughts and energy will transfer onto you and it will affect you. The same works the opposite way—your energy, thoughts, feelings and so on affects others. They will begin to act, behave, and react in a certain way based on the kind of energy they've received from you.

Again, it comes down to your own responsibility. Your thoughts affect other creatures' well being. The back and forth exchange of energy in intimate relationships is even more powerful. Please, give up the idea of forcing someone else to think like you because it is not going to work. And you don't want to control their thoughts because you can't! You cannot go against nature, no matter how hard you try.

Here's a great example of this kind of energy in action. I was at one of my Toastmasters club meetings when a guest came in to check out the club. Mary had never met me before and knew nothing about me. But after the meeting was over, she asked me if I had an ability to heal people. She could tell that this was my life's mission—to awaken human consciousness. She sensed it through the interconnectedness of energy. She felt it, and she was right on the money.

Another interesting example of energy connectedness is Facebook. Facebook is a social networking website and it can also be an ego boost sometimes! It's fun to stay in touch with everyone, and I love it when everyone checks in and writes updates. However, if you don't watch yourself, you can waste a whole lot of time online, which is unproductive.

One day I was online chatting with one of my friends and of course everyone was able to read it. Before I signed off, I announced that I was getting off of Facebook for the day because my work was waiting. As soon as I wrote that, I felt a great sense of relief, like the energy had been redirected. Just for the sake of the experiment, I checked back a few times and sure enough, there weren't many new entries on the news feed. As soon as I had let my friends know that I was going back to work, my energy affected others and they went back to work as well.

Your thoughts and your actions are magnetic, all through the invisible power of energy.

The Time Is Now! You Have the Answer!
Write the first thought that came to mind and share one action step you will take to create the result you want.　　Date:_____

_____

_____

_____

_____

Secret 49 | When a word comes out of your mouth, witness how it becomes a reality.

CONTEMPLATION: When you don't want to attract certain things into your life, don't ever let an invitation to them come out of your mouth. This is a guaranteed principle: your words do get heard. Once a statement or a word is out of your mouth, the universal energy takes it in, and it will materialize in your physical life. It's as simple as that

Before you attempt anything, always ask yourself the following:

- What specifically do I really want?
- Why do I want it? Listen to yourself breathing and witness the flow of air going through your nostrils.
- What is the outcome I really want from my desire? Stop, take a breath, and listen.

- Make sure that you are absolutely alone in a quiet, secluded place, without distractions and interruptions.

Write down the first thought that came into your mind and repeat it out loud quietly. How does it feel in your body?

1. If you feel a certain discomfort when you say it, it means that it is not true for you, or your inner world is not aligned with your outer world.
2. When you're certain, it will feel good in your body.
3. Only then write it down with certainty.
4. Only then say it to yourself with certainty.

I repeat—dreams do come true. What prevents you from realizing your dreams is doubt and fear. As Franklin Roosevelt said, "The only limit to our realization of tomorrow will be our doubts of today." Doubt comes from your ego, your mind. It cripples your existence.

Remember, the universal energy has an incredible way of working miracles, in connection with you, in both ways, seen and unseen. *Words have power, so think before you speak.* The answer is always present and within.

The Time Is Now! You Have the Answer!

Write the first thought that came to mind and share one action step you will take to create the result you want.   **DATE:** _____

Secret 50 | The universe gives you a message with every encounter and a new lesson to learn.

Contemplation: I confess that I'm the type of person who finds meaning in everything. Why else would I be here in a place where I have to find my own way, a place of free will? This search for meaning—the discovery and unwrapping of the messages of the universe—is the most beautiful part of the journey of life. Our parents played their role in the physical part of our creation, but the rest is up to us.

Do you think you are where you are right now because you have traveled through life and have gone through certain life events for a reason? Think about the fact that you're reading this book at this particular time in your life. You're writing your life story below. Literally, step-by-step. It is not a coincidence. You're now reading this book because you've searched through many other books, classes, and philosophies. At this moment, you're hoping you can finally find what you've been looking for. It's not an accident that I wrote this book and you're reading it right now. This is exactly what is supposed to happen.

Each one of you wants more than what you have right now. Maybe you don't have it because you don't really need it, or maybe you have not yet quite managed to align your energy with it. This is how the journey of life works; it happens only through perfection, a solid connection. My creation and existence are not accidents; neither is yours. It is meant to be.

What have you learned from your life up to this moment? What message do you want to send out to the universe for the rest of your physical existence? How open are you to receive, to hear the messages the universe, God, has for you? Stop to experience this moment! Stop running away, because it's impossible! This is what makes you unhappy.

The Time Is Now! You Have the Answer!
Write the first thought that came to mind and share one
action step you will take to create the result you want.   **Date:** _____

SECRET 51 | The beauty of the present moment is in opening up to the possibilities of tomorrow.

CONTEMPLATION: When you feel your life is going nowhere, or you are not sure where you're going, always look at the big picture and ask yourself, why do I feel this way?

You may feel one way on the surface, but there's a lot more happening than you can see at the moment. Later, you will discover that the universal energy, God, is working with you, in your own interest.

For instance, before my awakening, I was a hopeless romantic dreaming of a certain kind of man I wanted in my life, my own Prince Charming. It won't surprise you if I tell you I never met him. I was pretty stubborn back then. The man of my dreams did not exist—at least, not exactly the way I pictured him. As time passed, the universe introduced me to a similar, but different type of man who, I realized immediately, was exactly what I was looking for! During my awakening, I felt lonely because I couldn't encounter my "dream man." In the meantime, I was being exposed to the truth—by rediscovering, adjusting, and accepting what was right in front of me, but I couldn't see it. In reality, I was waking up to my true self.

Be patient with yourself. The truth may feel a bit unusual at the beginning. That will pass. The same basic scenario stands for any situation from your life—career, money, relationships, and so on!

Your judgments and feelings are temporary. They're guaranteed to change, just as you do! Depending on your ability to see, to recognize, and to practice acceptance, it's only a matter of time before what's good for you, and what's supposed to develop, shows up in your life. Allow nature to take its course.

The Time Is Now! You Have the Answer!

Write the first thought that came to mind and share one action step you will take to create the result you want.

Date: _____

CHANGE!

Change does not roll in on the wheels inevitability,
but comes through continuous struggle.

—Martin Luther King, Jr.

Secret 52 | When pain and suffering become unbearable, the human being changes and transforms.

Contemplation: Change and transformation are constant, but on a personal level, they happen at a different speed for each individual. Some travel through life easier, while others are resistant to the natural occurrence of change.

Most humans go through life without realizing life is passing them by. But how can anyone be happy when they resist evolution? How can one remain a caterpillar and not become a butterfly? In my own experience, most people I know want to be successful, happy, and make a difference in some way—they just don't know how.

Real transformation in most humans, unfortunately, seems to take place when one hits rock bottom such as a near death experience, as in my life, or losing everything you own, or getting sick with an incurable disease, or going through the death of a loved one, and so on. Until then, time just goes by. You're literally at your own mercy; you are the one that's keeping you stuck! Are you waiting for an unpleasant major life event to occur so you won't be responsible for waking yourself up?

For me, a major change and transformation happened just in time. I was spared so I could do something for myself, for others, and for the world I live in. I had to make a choice between life and death, and obviously I chose life because today I'm certain that my life is meaningful. What prevents people from success is an unwillingness to change—an unwillingness, really, to succeed. Success requires constant adjustment, change, and persistence.

Some people resist change for a long time. Guess what? Change is occurring regardless. The result is that time and life have passed them by; they find themselves unwilling, afraid, and tired to make a change. They think that change is impossible, so the only change they undergo is to grow old or to get sick and die. How sad to see a life wasted like that!

The Time Is Now! You Have the Answer!

Write the first thought that came to mind and share one action step you will take to create the result you want.

DATE: _____

SECRET 53 | You are afraid today because you don't want to repeat the mistakes you made yesterday.

CONTEMPLATION: The road to happiness is peaceful transformation. Life is an opportunity given to you. I know you have gone through a lot. It's up to you. Today is the day to make life work for you.

Life is a gamble, so keep rolling the dice until you hit it big, and even then you will need to keep up with it because you can lose all that you have gained. This is the temporary nature of life on Earth. As soon as you stop persevering, your energy will begin to stagnate, and you'll get stuck.

Then something will occur that'll make you feel sorry you ever stopped. This is God and the universal energy—it keeps testing you on a daily basis. The truth is that you can't stop. The mistakes you make will prepare you for the opportunities life presents. Keep going; keep trying.

On the other hand, there are some people who keep trying but are stuck on wildly unrealistic expectations for themselves. They're beating their heads against the wall. There's a time and place for everything. Balance is always the answer. Your age, for instance, is only a number to me. However, if you're trying to start a career as a professional rock star in your senior years, you are dreaming. (But you can always be the rock star to your family and friends!) I'm talking about focusing on yourself and authenticity, such as becoming a better husband, wife, father, mother, sister, a contributor to society, and so on. These are the things you don't want to stop trying to improve. I know, you may be tired of trying but as soon as you give up, you will sabotage your own well being and happiness.

Dare to keep trying. The mistakes you've made are the necessary steps to transformation on the journey of life. When you begin to feel that you cannot take another step, use it as a motivator to try again.

You are creating light, remember, and to create light you need the two opposite poles (the PRINCIPLE OF THE OPPOSITE ACTION©). When you feel you've failed (the negative pole), counteract it with your effort to try again (the positive pole), and you'll create light and fulfillment.

The Time Is Now! You Have the Answer!
Write the first thought that came to mind and share one action step you will take to create the result you want.   DATE:_____

_____

_____

_____

_____

SECRET 54 | Your transformation feels easy, free-flowing, and natural.

CONTEMPLATION: Some people I know have gotten so much into Eastern teachings and all kinds of practices or cults that it has changed their behavior in a strange way. They are trying hard to learn all the different methods, all the different phrases.

Note that another way your ego controls you is when you try hard to appear highly intelligent or philosophical to others. I know a lot of people like that. They want to appear "cool" to others because they feel so un-cool about themselves deep inside. Some even seem to take pleasure in looking or sounding weird. But, you know, that gives a bad name to some practices and teachings that are beneficial, and it may put off people who simply want to awaken.

I'll never forget when I went to check out a Buddhist Temple in Los Angeles and was welcomed by a woman who was taking care of the place. She was an older woman, a really sweet lady who had not washed herself in a few days but told me what meditation had done for her. She took herself, and meditation in general, way too seriously. If meditation had really awakened her she would have known that she literally stank. She smelled so bad that it was hard for me to stand near her so that we could talk!

Everything you do is for yourself, for your well being, not to impress anyone but yourself. Remember, you don't have to become someone else. When going through life, especially when you introduce a new daily routine, if it feels uneasy, listen to your body telling you that there's something you need to change, to readjust, because whatever you're doing may not be good for you at this particular time. It's the real you that you're getting in touch with—the you that already exists!

Today, I'm stunned by some people's attitudes. Despite the current economic crisis and the lessons we need to learn from it, some people remain unchanged. They did not get the message from God. God's message to human nature is to change its selfish, corruptive, and greedy ways! It's shocking to see how so many people can be in such turmoil but don't recognize that if they merely change their ways, everything will change around them! How stubborn can that be?

The Time Is Now! You Have the Answer!
Write the first thought that came to mind and share one
action step you will take to create the result you want.   DATE:_____

SECRET 55 | Control your selfish desires and begin today to practice the Principle of Giving©.

CONTEMPLATION: The reason why people feel unhappy in the material world is because of their desire to receive for themselves alone, also known as selfishness. For instance, many people consider their financial donation to a church or a charity the fulfillment of a duty. But it is not a duty. It's a joy. It's an opening; a freeing; a letting go. Become aware, in each moment, of the natural need to release through giving. Each one of us is blessed with it. It's just that you may have not yet awakened to it. It's part of our natural makeup.

Human nature is selfish; that's a fact. For instance, some parents insist that their child becomes a doctor, or a lawyer, because this is what the parent wants—it may not be a matter of what the child wants. (Of course, most parents want the best for their kids and want them to be happy.)

I am also practical. We live in a selfish world. Stand up for yourself to keep from being eaten alive. Above all, there is a fine order in which the infinite intelligence, God, works—it's called balance.

God is abundance. We are created by God (or Nature, if you'd like). God is within, which means you too are abundance. If you do not share that abundance, it stagnates. Your abundance, if not shared, starts to rot within. It goes against Nature. To become in tune with God (Nature) is to open up and release what you have been naturally blessed with—abundance. Begin to practice daily what I call the PRINCIPLE OF GIVING©.

PRINCIPLE OF GIVING©

When you interfere with the natural release and exchange of energy through giving you start rotting inside like overripe apples that fell from the tree: never picked, shared, or enjoyed. This is when misery and unhappiness start to appear. Human beings are blessed with freedom of

expression. Freedom is about openness in the energy flow of exchange through giving. Your energy channels are in need of free-flowing energy. This is what's required for a healthy body, mind, and soul connection. When you hold off the natural need for release through giving you block the energy. Learn to always first give to yourself. Develop your self knowledge to be able to give of the "genuine you" to others. Give yourself the gift and practice of meditation. Live your life in this present moment! Take action! This is how you apply unconditional love through giving.

In my past, I have suffered tremendously from my selfish nature. Today, I have turned around 180 degrees. At the end of each day I now make it a point to ask myself: What did I give back today in exchange for all the food I am eating, all the air I am breathing and all the beauty I am surrounded by living in such a beautiful home?

How fair is it to accept such gifts from the universe and to not give back on a daily basis? If I know of someone who is unhappy and who needs help, I often give the gift of my teaching and coaching skills. I talk to that person free of charge, as a friend, within certain professional boundaries. It has been such a joy to see people transform their lives right in front of my eyes—like watching new flowers sprouting from the wintry earth!

Your true nature is abundance. Develop a habit to share your God given abundance with others on a daily basis. It is an incredible way of releasing your positive energy into the world and it feels really good. It has changed my life and self esteem for the better and it has made me who I am today.

The PRINCIPLE OF GIVING© works best when applied daily. When you practice the PRINCIPLE OF GIVING© I guarantee you a life of happiness and well being.

The Time Is Now! You Have the Answer!
Write the first thought that came to mind and share one action step you will take to create the result you want.   DATE:_____

Secret 56 | Keep giving without being concerned about receiving.

CONTEMPLATION: It is part of human nature to expect a return for what you've done or given. You are stimulated to work hard when you know that you'll be rewarded for it. In our day to day dealings everything's an exchange, but a temporary exchange. You get it and it's gone. Then you don't have much left and you're unhappy again. You keep searching for something more fulfilling, for permanence.

Energy exchange, on the contrary, is exciting, authentic, and lasting. Giving opens the door to abundance. But when you start putting conditions in the mind, thinking about what you're going to receive, it creates energy blocks. For instance, I know individuals who always think about what they're going to get back. They work hard and are concerned about the success of the project they're working on. In the back of their mind, however, their number one priority is what they are going to receive. They subconsciously create an energy obstacle that stifles the quality of their performance. If your number one priority is strictly about receiving, you will not be able to connect to *The Source of Wealth in You*™. Thoughts are powerful; they can create one of two things: (1) a barrier or (2) a release of energy.

A positive thought creates good energy. A selfish thought stems from the ego that always needs to be fed, which short circuits the creation of light.

When you operate from Source you don't have to think of rewards; they are already there—it's pure abundance. The inner abundant reservoir will give you anything you want. It is stable, reliable, and everlasting. Ask yourself daily, how can I begin to give unconditionally in a world where I exist under conditions?

When you give from your authentic Source, only then you will receive back the same and it will last. Money is not a true Source of Wealth. When you think of it as such, you bring misery, confusion, anger, and fear into your life. However, money is very important in today's living standards.

Money and spirituality, in my teachings, go hand-in-hand. True happiness and material riches are interdependent. Happiness is a prerequisite for material riches. I call it balance—it always starts from the inside out.

What do I have to do exactly to operate from my real Source? It depends on how you look at it. A balanced point of view would give you a more realistic outlook. By being born into this world, you took on a responsibility to really make a contribution, a difference, and to give. For example, to some of the people who have looked to me for help, I have suggested fostering or adopting a child or a pet. You know that your money isn't going with you when you die. What better way could there be than to rediscover yourself by becoming a great example and to help another creature survive, to thrive in this world?

The Time Is Now! You Have the Answer!
Write the first thought that came to mind and share one action step you will take to create the result you want.　　Date:_____

Secret 57 | Transform your desires for your own and the benefit of all.

CONTEMPLATION: This is another characteristic of the human condition: no matter what you have, you want more. You keep looking; you keep wanting. Human beings are victims of constant desire.

Remember, you cannot have it all because you're human; that's your form for this lifetime. This constant desire is both a curse and a blessing. It's a curse if you continually want things you don't need or things that are not good for you. (It wasn't for nothing that the early Christians included greed, gluttony, lust, and envy in their list of the "Seven Deadly Sins.")

Awareness will help you detach yourself from your constant desires, and you'll become happier. True abundance is your birthright when you are connected to Source.

Your desire is also a blessing. A desire for success and taking action is required to succeed in life. Success in the material world is possible if you continuously use your desire to succeed and to do well in all areas of life. To reach the pinnacle of success, make your compulsive desires and addictive human tendencies work for you. Practice daily the PRINCIPLE OF SELECTIVE DESIRE©.

Barriers occur because there are so many choices out there. Keep in mind, when something seems complicated it's your responsibility to simplify it. For instance, if a project or an issue seems too big, dissect it; cut it into small projects and tackle the small projects one at a time.

Life always works out for the best. Keep this in mind and you'll succeed. There's always the possibility that you might miss the materialization of a particular desire—but if that happens, there's a lesson for you to learn from. Perhaps you needed to fall, so you can learn a very important lesson. Without it, you would not have learned it.

The Time Is Now! You Have the Answer!
Write the first thought that came to mind and share one action step you will take to create the result you want. ♩DATE:_____

DISCOVER THE BALANCE

Life is a promise; fulfill it.

—Mother Teresa

Life is like riding a bicycle.
To keep your balance you must keep moving.

—Albert Einstein

Secret 58 | Life on Earth is only a passing moment, a tiny part of the big picture—of eternity.

Contemplation: Human beings are addicted to drama and to the adrenaline rush it gives. But that wears out quickly, doesn't it? It's quick and temporary.

Whatever is happening in your life right now is bound to change and that's guaranteed. This is the nature of life, people, events, and so on. Life's crises are guaranteed to pass. The "bad times" do not last.

I remember, one time, when I was sick and given a medication with an unpleasant side effect: it made me nauseated. I had a choice: to either throw up to get a temporary relief, or to trick my mind so I could keep it in my system long enough to benefit from it. The doctor had warned me about the reaction. When I took the medicine I felt a lot worse than I thought I would. I was tempted to get the medication out of my system to temporarily relieve myself from the nausea.

I sat at my desk in agony, close to an hour, thinking about what to do. I came up with a solution: I went to bed, lay on my back, and started to consciously breathe. Eventually I calmed down from breathing properly and worn out from the agony I was in. I fell asleep and woke up two hours later feeling refreshed.

This is exactly how life works. Create a trick for the mind in that particular moment, when the world tumbles upon you, to get through some difficult times. The same counts for major life events. When in crisis, remember what you read here and use the life tools from this book. The Secrets, Principles, Affirmations, and Exercises in this book are the tools to help you get through it all.

Remember to take a specific action toward resolution. Life and its painful events are temporary. Only the truth remains forever. Stay in touch with the truth that's in you.

The Time Is Now! You Have the Answer!

Write the first thought that came to mind and share one
action step you will take to create the result you want.　　🦅 DATE: _____

SECRET 59 | Life is a continuous journey without an ending or destination. You're forever!

CONTEMPLATION: A friend of mine named Jacky went on a Caribbean cruise last winter. I knew she had a wonderful time and was itching to tell me all about it, so I asked her how it went. "Well, we didn't get anywhere," she laughed. "We started out in Miami and after seven days of sailing, what the heck, we were right back in Miami again!"

She was just joking, of course; Jacky had a blast on her vacation, but it brings up something I notice in people quite a lot: many find it hard to understand the concept of a voyage without destination. Enjoy the journey so it becomes a fun process about peaceful transformation that leads to happiness. Refuse to fight with yourself. Let go of expectations. Allow transformation to naturally take its course. Surrender to perfection and to the energy you're made of to allow transformation to take its course.

On my journey, I had tried to cut corners in many ways. But shortcuts don't work; they're impossible. I finally had to painfully surrender, with the understanding that I was the only one who can do it for myself and for my own sake. When it comes to change, a teacher, a coach, or a support group may give you the motivation and encouragement you need, but you need to rely on yourself and to look within. To connect to your authentic self, dip into the wisdom you have within. Once you get in touch with the real you—the energy that you are, the soul, the spirit—only then does each day become more beautiful and meaningful.

Take a deep breath and realize that you are a traveler—but there is no "set destination." There doesn't have to be; it's really not all up to you anyway. On a deeper level we exist and co-exist in unity with the universal intelligence, God, and the cosmos. Remember, you're not the only one "driving the car!" Get in the backseat once in awhile and enjoy the ride! It's all about the moment, this moment. But just in case you still feel unsure about it, know that you will always start from yourself and will return to yourself. The journey is its own reward.

Always look at the big picture. You're a lot more than what you "think" you are. You're more than what you're aware of at the moment. You are energy that has been and always will be here. Energy has no destination, only physical matter does. Matter diminishes and disintegrates, but the real you will never end. You are forever!

The Time Is Now! You Have the Answer!
Write the first thought that came to mind and share one action step you will take to create the result you want.   🖋Date:_____

_____

_____

_____

_____

Secret 60 | Acknowledge what your life is worth to you.

CONTEMPLATION: Balance and success go hand-in-hand. When you're successful, you're happy. Happiness is a prerequisite for success. Suppose you consider yourself a success, but you do not have balance in your life. Without balance, there isn't authentic success. Maybe you're living your life without a purpose or feel you've spent a large part of it unhappy. Now that some time has passed, you're afraid that it's too late to change your life.

The truth is that it's never too late. You can find examples of people who first experienced success in their sixties. But why would you want to wait that long to only enjoy success here, on Earth, for a short while? I know that the "time is now," at any age!

To balance your life, take some time for yourself and by yourself to begin to fully experience and to realize that you are an energy force. You are an instrumental part of the universal energy field. When you awaken and realize that this is who you are, authentic success will reveal itself to you.

Today is the day to embark on a wonderful journey of discovery, a journey that reveals why you are here—because your life is waiting. Do not take for granted the gift of life given to you; that would not be fair to you or to the world that you live in. You don't want to be a taker and discovering or creating your life's meaning and purpose will require you to give.

If you have not been a giver before, become one. Make giving a priority in your life and you will rediscover a whole new world opening up to you: your life's meaning and purpose. As soon as you take a step to do so, the clouds will clear and the doubt will dissipate.

Write down what I call I RELEASE THE ABUNDANCE THAT I AM AFFIRMATION© and look at it nightly right before you fall asleep, and as soon as you open your eyes in the morning.

I RELEASE THE ABUNDANCE THAT I AM AFFIRMATION©

> "There is a reason for everything. My life has meaning and purpose. I now simply give of myself. I'm discovering new ways to give all the time. This is now the way of my existence. I give good energy to others. I now accept others the way they are because they're like me—human. I give without being concerned about receiving. I am a giver. It's such a release!"

The Time Is Now! You Have the Answer!
Write the first thought that came to mind and share one
action step you will take to create the result you want.   🖋 DATE: _____

_____

_____

_____

_____

SECRET 61 | Life on Earth is like a dream. You cannot allow yourself to take it too seriously.

CONTEMPLATION: I live my life here, on Earth, with the understanding that I have no guarantees as to its reality.

Suppose that life on Earth is nothing but a dream. For example, the reality may be that I died when I fell asleep last night and took the "Diana right now" body that I am in this moment. There might be others mourning for me, really suffering my loss somewhere else, but I'm not even aware of it because of the new form I took after my death last night—the form I am in this very moment.

By the way, I truly am still uncertain if I'm dead or alive, having experienced death—or was it a dream?—in 2007. What are your guarantees in the material (physical) world? There are guarantees I wrote throughout this book and they're few.

There's a second part to my dream theory to help you deal with life. Become a dreamer now, in your current form, in the material (physical) world. I am a passionate dreamer, and what I dream about becomes a reality. By dreaming and creating it in my mind I've made it so real to me that I've sent a crystal clear message to the universe. The universe took me seriously, within God's boundaries, always. I honestly have seen the impossible happen in my life through creating, dreaming, and imagination—all combined with action. And I haven't been afraid of it either because I know it's all just "like a dream."

Becoming a dreamer is essential to creating your life. All you need is to act upon it so your dreams can materialize with tangible results. As long as you initiate and act upon your dreams, imaginations, and creations, while remaining true to yourself, they will be realized and materialized.

The Time Is Now! You Have the Answer!
Write the first thought that came to mind and share one action step you will take to create the result you want.   **DATE:** _____

SECRET 62 | What you need is right in front of you. As soon as you wake up you'll recognize it.

CONTEMPLATION: How many times have you realized, looking back on the course of events, that what you had to do to get somewhere or to accomplish something in life was right in front of you after all, but you just couldn't see it?

Religion teaches that we come from good, and that is absolutely true for me. Anything negative or unbalanced is an anomaly; that is, if something is off kilter, it needs to be realigned with the natural beauty and balance that is in you.

Life is complicated enough, but the mind often puts blinders on and leads us into more confusion and suffering. What if you remove the blinders? What if you try to see and recognize what's right in front of you?

Wherever you are right now, in this moment and at this stage of your life, there is a reason for it. It means that everything that's in tune with your being is right here, right now. There is a saying that the person you marry is right around the corner from where you live. What you need is right here.

The universal intelligence, God, is in tune with your needs. Stop and take the time to notice what may not appear to be obvious to you. If you cannot see it, give it some time. This is not to say that you'll always get what you want, but I know you'll get what you need. If you don't receive it at this particular time, make some adjustments in your life, or in your way of communicating with Source. Maybe some time has to pass so you can become ready for it. Then you'll notice it; it's right here and in front of you.

The following is an exercise that leads to insight and awareness. I call it the RHYTHM OF YOUR HEART AWAKENING MEDITATION©.

RHYTHM OF YOUR HEART AWAKENING MEDITATION©

Lie down on your left side. Extend the left arm and place your head on it instead of a pillow and adjust it until you feel comfortable. You will be able to hear your heartbeat very well. Breathe and listen to your heartbeat for ten minutes. If this position feels uncomfortable to you, use a large size clock. Lie down on your back. Breathe consciously while listening to the arms of the moving clock sound. Notice each second/sound it makes. Keep listening for ten minutes. Simple! Awaken to what's in front of you and recognize it so you can develop your intuition and gain more insight. By becoming aware of your own heartbeat you'll start to notice some of the other details of life.

The Time Is Now! You Have the Answer!
Write the first thought that came to mind and share one
action step you will take to create the result you want. ❥DATE:_____

_____

_____

SECRET 63 | What is my soul's mission for this particular lifetime on Earth?

CONTEMPLATION: Most people don't want to dig deeper into themselves. They're afraid of what they might find. Living on the surface, however, isn't meaningful, but it might seem like an easy way to live. Remember, anything of worth does not come easy. I do not judge, blame, or have anything against these types of people, but what's the point of going through life without ever discovering the mission of their souls for this particular lifetime? What would happen if we had to come back here, on Earth, to start all over again? I would say, why not discover and live by it this time around so you have something even more exciting to look forward to—transcending to a different level of existence?

Today, I see my friends in their teens searching. They are really wise. I'm blown away by the mottos they write on their Facebook page. The teenagers have had it too—with material possessions, broken homes, greed, corruption, the economic crisis, and the conditions of today's volatile world. Times are changing, and the teenagers are taking an active part in this change.

There is a group of young professionals who are now actively searching, regardless of their busy schedules and juggling around tons of daily responsibilities.

Others, however, have decided that it might take a lifetime to discover what they came here to do, so they're "kind of" searching. They sometimes take a whole lifetime because they've preprogrammed their computer software, their mind, that they will not be able to find out what they came here to do and subconsciously keep sabotaging it.

Another kind of group strives for success and works tirelessly in the material world, but find themselves with not a lot to do when the kids leave home. They're left with some investment to use for the future—for travel, retirement, and so on. What about the 20 or 30 years they may have left to live? This is when they finally have time to look for more, to look within. But they feel that something always has been missing in their life. There is definitely some valuable lifetime spent focusing on the material world, but not enough food has been supplied to their souls. Stress has been the leading factor in their lives. This is one of the reasons that most people look older than their biological age. Then, they spend lots of money to look young, but stress is very hard to erase, even when they can afford the best cosmetic products and services. Start taking care of yourself today. Remember, you're always a priority.

Now, take a moment to write down this affirmation—I call it MY SOUL'S MISSION AFFIRMATION©—on an index card or somewhere you know you will see it every night before you fall asleep and every morning as soon as you open your eyes, and say it aloud.

MY SOUL'S MISSION AFFIRMATION©

> "I am energy! I am a soul residing and manifesting itself through my physical body where I exist temporarily. My body is guaranteed to die. My soul will continue to live, to swim in the sea of universal energy, to embrace, and to interact with other souls in the unending dance of life. But I must complete what I came here to do! I came here to fulfill a purpose. I am now being awakened to my life's purpose. I am living my mission on Earth so I can be forever released from human bondage—from the cycle of birth and death, pain and suffering."

The Time Is Now! You Have the Answer!
Write the first thought that came to mind and share one action step you will take to create the result you want. 🙟DATE:_____

SECRET 64 | Life is about simplicity. Release the obsession to try so hard in life!

CONTEMPLATION: As soon as you stop obsessing over an issue, a relationship, or life in general, the answers will come to you and a resolution will take place.

When you want something so badly that you worry about it and can think of nothing else, everything goes against you. Your energy is charged with fear, worries, and desperation that interrupts and blocks the perfect flow of the universal energy. The two main reasons you're full of wants and desires are:

1. You're not yet aware of the abundance that you are that is already available within. It's still unfamiliar to you.
2. You feel insecure (but this is not who you really are). You may feel worthless, so you look for more to fill the void within

You may have what you need but your desires persist because you're human. You keep trying to become more successful, to make more money, and you keep looking for more love, joy, and happiness. Human beings are not easily satisfied and always think they need more. Why do you want more?

- You're living a life of illusion created by your own mind, or by others.
- You're asleep—blind to the abundance within and the beauty of God all around you.
- You have not yet discovered who you are and what you came here to do.

Well, how about shifting gears for a while? In fact, put your gearshift into neutral. Release the obsessions and control your desires. This is the answer to your happiness. Today, reprogram your mind's computer software to the following:

- Abundance is yours and you're the Source of Wealth.
- Let go of the issue you're struggling with to create some space for the perfect universal energy to readjust and to do its work. Letting go is a great way to allow the answer and renewed energy to come in.

How many important scientific discoveries and breakthroughs have been made this way, by people who were able to relax for a while and think of something entirely different, or of nothing at all?

For example, recall the story of Archimedes, the Greek mathematician, who idly pondered a problem as he was getting into his bath (and realized weight displacement was his answer). Or, Sir Isaac Newton who was relaxing under an apple tree when, so the story goes, an apple fell from above and bumped him on the head which gave him the opportunity to mull over the principle of gravity. When you leave the problem alone for a while and detach from it, you will create space for the answers to be redirected toward you.

Relax and let the universal energy do its work. Take a day off today. Then, when presented with an answer, continue toward its realization by taking action.

The Time Is Now! You Have the Answer!

Write the first thought that came to mind and share one action step you will take to create the result you want.   DATE:_____

SECRET 65 | Life is about working smart.

CONTEMPLATION: Life is a wheel. In life coaching, we use the concept of the WHEEL OF LIFE. The WHEEL OF LIFE looks like a pie divided into seven different categories such as the SEVEN AREAS OF YOUR LIFE—career; money; health/beauty/fitness; friends/family/relationships; personal development; fun and recreation; and physical environment. You are at the center, at the hub of the WHEEL OF LIFE. Also, each of the categories of the WHEEL OF LIFE can be taken separately and made into a separate wheel and divided again into subcategories, depending on what you feel needs to be addressed. But you're always at the center.

Take a look at the drawing of the WHEEL OF LIFE in the Glossary and using a scale from 1 to 10—level 1 is the closest to the center and level 10 is at the periphery of the wheel—mark the level you feel you're at for each area of your life. When you connect the marks of all areas, you can literally see the balance or the imbalance of the WHEEL, meaning your life.

The WHEEL OF LIFE is often out of balance. Just like an unaligned car wheel, it will make your car hard to drive, or even impossible, until you get it balanced. This happens when you've neglected getting a tune up. How about a flat tire? Can you drive with a flat tire? Try it, but you and I know that we can't. A flat tire, or anything "flat," for that matter, represents a weak life foundation.

There are people who work all the time but seem to keep chasing their own tail. Working smart includes the following steps:

1. Work with a qualified coach for three months. Isn't it what personal trainers do? In my own experience I was in my best physical shape when I shot my first movie and that was the time I had a personal trainer. It made a huge difference in the way I looked for the filming.
2. Read and write in this book. This is an official initiation to the journey.
3. Re-create your life—create a blueprint for your new life by setting up a solid foundation. Ask the questions and answer them.
4. Set up one major goal for each month.

5. Take baby steps; dissect each goal.

6. Slowly allow yourself to get used to the "new you."

7. Take responsibility and remember that you don't need anyone to babysit you or to tell you what to do.

What is more important: To work hard or to work smart; to invest in yourself or to invest in something else? What will you do today to change yourself and to break the cycle of making the same mistakes over and over until you get too tired or motivated to make a change?

The Time Is Now! You Have the Answer!
Write the first thought that came to mind and share one action step you will take to create the result you want.   **Date:** _____

_____

_____

_____

_____

Secret 66 | Life can become a vicious circle.

Contemplation: Life goes on. Humans divide, subdivide, judge, label everything and keep going around in circles. But if that's happening, something is broken. There's a disconnect somewhere.

What is broken and disconnected here is the self. For example, you keep changing intimate or business partners to only find out years later you got yourself into the same situation and encountered the same issues; you spent years of your life discovering what you already knew. Then you shrug and say, "Time flies." You keep changing jobs, or careers, only to find that the same circumstances appear over and over again.

Unless you've made an investment in yourself, there's no way out of the vicious circle of repeating the mistakes, of doing the same thing over and over again. This is what we call chasing one's tail—running after something you see wagging in the mist ahead only to discover that it's nothing but the movement of your own back end.

What is the reason for all this circularity? Resistance to change, unhappiness with yourself, deteriorating physical health, being lost, confused, or stubborn—the list can go on and on. So what can you do today to stop the vicious cycle?

- Become consciously aware of the mistakes you keep making; learn from them and catch yourself right on the spot before you make them again.
- Don't try to control others; take control of your life. Focus and control yourself.

The Time Is Now! You Have the Answer!
Write the first thought that came to mind and share one action step you will take to create the result you want.   DATE: _____

SECRET 67 | Life is about beauty—representing and creating it by taking care of your inner and outer self.

CONTEMPLATION: I value beauty and I know I'm not alone. The balance between inner and outer beauty is extremely attractive. It makes you look and feel young because you operate from stability, which represents inner peace.

Genuine beauty comes from the inside. It's different from the sort of beauty cosmetics companies, popular magazines, and TV shows purvey. It is the sort of beauty that sometimes shines forth from the faces of old people or from those who have been terribly scarred. You can see such kindness, empathy, understanding, and human joy in people's faces that they appear radiantly beautiful. That is the sort of beauty I value most because it's real. For many people, however, outer beauty remains only skin deep.

I remember the time, before my transformation a few years ago, when all I saw was the negative qualities and faults of others. It was the true mirror effect: I was seeing myself in them. I was disgusted with myself, not with others. I was miserable but hated others for it. Today, when I see angry, unhappy people out there it reminds me of those times. I know exactly what is happening within. When they are open to it, I guide them to look inside themselves, to see for themselves, but often they have put up walls and barriers. Most people cannot see inside themselves or do not want to; some may not even know what I'm talking about.

Life is different for me now and transformation is possible. It's the only way. Today, every time I catch myself finding fault in others, I stop. Now, I'm aware of myself and I catch myself before I cause damage. Each time this happens it's a blessing because it allows me to see how human and flawed I still am and that I cannot stop working on improving myself to meaningfully exist in this world. Remember, you and I are here on Earth, an imperfect place, a place that we can make better and more beautiful.

The Time Is Now! You Have the Answer!
Write the first thought that came to mind and share one action step you will take to create the result you want.   ❥Date:_____

SECRET 68 | Live your life with pure intentions.

CONTEMPLATION: To me, intention is related to Karma (aka the PRINCIPLE OF CAUSE AND EFFECT©). Do you ever stop to consider your intention before you say or do something? Do you ask yourself what kind of development you foresee and why?

A pure intention naturally leads to the same kind of communication, which can save you lots of disappointment and anger toward others. Anytime your intentions are less than pure, the other person knows about it. All humans are blessed with an inexplicable sense of knowingness—what we call intuition. Some people have a stronger intuitive sense than others and are exceptionally good at sensing what has not been spoken and seeing what cannot be seen and knowing the unknowable. But even if your intuition is not highly developed you can tell if someone is lying or if there's anything fake or phony.

Remember, you're a soul and your soul knows the truth. The Greek word for "soul" is "psyche," and on a psychic level we're connected, all one—we are intermingled parts of the united universal energy field. Only on a physical level we're separated—black and white, rich and poor, young and old, and so on. So, just like you, other people have what Ernest Hemingway called "a built in bullshit detector" and can always tell when something's less than pure.

Purifying your thoughts and intentions, as well as your body, will not only clarify your mind but will also send a clear message to others. It will make life so much easier!

The Time Is Now! You Have the Answer!
Write the first thought that came to mind and share one
action step you will take to create the result you want. DATE:_____

Secret 69 | Producing works of beauty, wonder, and value would make your life meaningful.

Contemplation: The above statement can easily become your life's mission, but be very simple and specific or else it can just become a string of words, a daydream. The work you do does not have to be a Shakespearean play, a Rembrandt painting, or a computer innovation that will make you as rich as Bill Gates. It can be modest and humble; to better your life and the lives of others.

For example, practice becoming the person you want to be (a person who is not angry, for instance, or a person who's always on time) by being that person only one day a week. You can do that! And if you can be that person for one day, you can be it for two days, then three days, then every day.

You can choose any one area from the Seven Areas of Your Life. Be very specific so the universe can receive a clear message from you. Always start and remain simple when trying to break a habit and learn a new one. You need stability in order to establish a new character trait—walk before you can run—so start small.

My favorite example of a work of great value for both yourself and for society as a whole is raising a child who is centered, loved, and emotionally stable enough to continue the process for generations to come. Is there a more beautiful, wonderful gift to the world than this? Share with me what great works you have in store.

The Time Is Now! You Have the Answer!

Write the first thought that came to mind and share one
action step you will take to create the result you want.　　🌿Date:_____

_____

_____

_____

_____

Secret 70 | Create balance and understanding by looking at the two sides of the same coin.

CONTEMPLATION: Success in life and clear communication with others will start to appear when you make it a habit to ask yourself: What does that mean other than what it appears to be?

There are many different ways of looking at an object, a concept, a memory, a dream, a business deal, a person, and so on. I only ask you to look at the two sides. If you try more than two there's a chance you'll start obsessing by overthinking.

Conflicts arise when two people can't see beyond their own viewpoints. What does it look like in a different light, in a different context or from a different viewpoint? Finding a new way of looking at life is about discovering your own truth and what works for you. It's about getting in touch with your authenticity, the real Source.

The different roles we play in life in the material world make it harder for us to communicate. We are happy when we share our positive energies with each other but even in the best of circumstances most people have difficulty communicating clearly.

For instance, the role you play in this moment can feel restrictive to you and to the person with whom you're communicating. You may feel uncomfortable speaking directly. Each of you is gifted with strong intuition and deep within you know what is true for you. You'll be able to communicate more smoothly and honestly when you're in touch with your authentic self, constantly drawing from Source.

Remember, what you're hearing can always mean something else to someone else's ears. When you feel uncomfortable, when there's still something bothering you, keep asking the questions. Clarify what's being said to reach a balanced perspective and ultimately a balanced resolution.

The Time Is Now! You Have the Answer!
Write the first thought that came to mind and share one action step you will take to create the result you want.   DATE:_____

SECRET 71 | Spirituality and science coexist in balance.

CONTEMPLATION: Science and spirituality go hand-in-hand. Science cannot exist without spirituality, and vice versa. I support and promote both equally. We are living in a global world, an East meets West world. Meditation is the truth. That's been said many times, but a lot of people still don't know much about meditation. Most people have not yet found the way to connect with themselves.

First, meditation is not focused thought. If it feels that way to you, you're trying too hard. The real you—the soul—is pure. When you see people doing things the hard way all the time, it means they're running away from themselves. They're controlled by their mind exclusively and are far away from the truth.

The truth will come to you. The human emotions and insecurities cloud the truth within, but when you become the truth, you'll then be too smart for any destructive thoughts. It's always a struggle for control—between your mind and soul.

Before you begin to meditate regularly you want to be in reasonably good physical health. Meditation is impossible when you're not feeling well, or your blood pressure is elevated, or you're sick. Many people take medications to correct physical problems or to get enough sleep and I am not against that; many rely on medical science simply to survive until they awaken. But even then some medications will still be needed. Seek balance in the dosage of the medications you take. You might not need to take as much as you do at the moment. It depends on when and at which stage of your life you began a daily personal development routine and how much baggage has been accumulated by then.

Teach your children healthy habits to prevent diseases. Explain meditation to your children and how it works as early as possible. Give the gift of meditation to your child. Encourage physical exercise that leads to a healthy night's sleep, rather than teaching them (by example) how to put themselves to sleep with alcohol or sleeping pills.

In science and medicine, as in everything else, always seek balance. Be careful with what you put into your body and take only the medications that are a must. Take care of yourself, get second and third opinions, and become knowledgeable about your health and healthcare provider. In today's world not every doctor is trustworthy. Finding a good and honest doctor can become a challenge. But, remember, you're worth it. Awaken and you'll know exactly who and what is good for you. It all depends on how much you care about yourself, and how much you want to feel good and how much time you're willing to invest in yourself. It's about you!

The Time Is Now! You Have the Answer!
Write the first thought that came to mind and share one
action step you will take to create the result you want.   🌰DATE:_____

SECRET 72 | There is a perfect balance between science and spirituality—a survival tool for the material world.

CONTEMPLATION: I might be the only author who supports both medicine and spirituality. I call it modern spirituality. What worked 3,500 years ago just doesn't cut it today. The cosmos is different and its effects on humans are stronger. Surviving in the hectic world we live in without medicine or science is impossible. Spirituality alone cannot exist without science. The balance between the two determines your success and well being.

To attain well being, always take care of your physical ailments, especially the ones that are hereditary. See your doctor regularly. To draw effortlessly from your inner Source of Wealth you absolutely must take care of the physical body (your outer self). We cannot blame people's physical ailments on spiritual shortcomings. We live in the material world and that's its nature—full of all kinds of diseases and flaws. Are we going to let this interfere with our spirit and our spiritual evolution? You know the answer.

I know it sounds different than what you've heard before, but this is the type of spirituality I promote—the modern world awakening. You cannot make a physically sick body connect with its true nature—its soul.

I recommend the following:

- Look at the obvious—the body. If you have high blood pressure, diabetes, asthma, etc., find the medication that's right for you and treat your body.

- Next, dig in for the real stuff and treat your energy bodies—the root of all physical illness—through energy healing. Only then will you have the strength to look for the treasure within—*The Source of Wealth in You*™. Seek a highly qualified specialist to heal your energy bodies once and forever. Before you even get on the road to enlightenment, you must heal your energy bodies first.

- Eventually, things will start turning around. But you need your body, which is the home for your soul, during this particular lifetime on Earth. In the material world your soul needs a home.

- Lastly, always look at the big picture. When the mind, body, and soul connect in the material world you will be relieved of pain and suffering most of the time. At the same time you're preparing for the next stage of your existence. The mind-body-soul connection at this stage of your life is very important. Your current life is the foundation for what's in store for you in the evolution of your soul. It all depends on you, always, so accept it.

The Time Is Now! You Have the Answer!

Write the first thought that came to mind and share one action step you will take to create the result you want.

DATE: _____

You're the Source of Wealth

The gold mine within
is the only place to look for happiness.

—Diana DeMar

I searched for God and found only myself.
I searched for myself and found only God.

—Sufi Proverb

SECRET 73 | You're the Source of incredible wealth—a mine full of gold.

CONTEMPLATION: The search for joy and happiness is an ongoing process. The yearning for it is constant. The following are some of the reasons:

1. Most people choose to remain unhappy. They take no actual steps toward attaining fulfillment in their lives.

2. In the search for happiness, people seldom look within but focus outside of themselves.

For example, looking back a few years ago, when I felt unhappy I was a shopping junkie the same exact way a drug addict needs a fix. I needed to shop to try to fill the emptiness inside of me. Those were the times when I thought I really needed a new outfit, new sneakers, a new piece of furniture, a new iPod, a bigger external hard drive to protect my life—oops, my data!—from being lost, and so on. I know this was not just me; it was true for a whole lot of people (before the world economic crisis). And it's not just shopping—it's anything people do to keep from looking inside themselves.

Another barrier to people's happiness is the fear of success, or fear of expressing themselves, or surrendering to true love, and so on. People are afraid. You don't know what you'll find if you look within to search for the answers. It's an unknown territory so who would dare to go in there? It's easier to stay on the outside but you will spend your whole life unhappy.

The truth is that you're a gold mine! The gold mine within is the only place to look for happiness. Equip yourself with the tools to match your craftsmanship and dare to go on an adventure. This is how you can live a fulfilling life. Once you've attained the tools and are properly equipped you can perform fearlessly out in the world. Other people will look at you and they'll see greatness—they'll see a lion, an eagle, a Cleopatra, an Einstein, or a Montezuma. There is one of those in each of you. I promise.

The Time Is Now! You Have the Answer!
Write the first thought that came to mind and share one
action step you will take to create the result you want. 🌱Date:_____

_____

_____

_____

_____

Secret 74 | God is The Source of Wealth in You™.

Contemplation: In the material world we live in we use names and categories to label everything. Even God has been given different names so that we can be judgmental—so that we can say, "Your God is not as good as my God," as if God was a college football team!

Humans constantly judge. "Judgmental" is made up of two words: "judge" and "mental." Think about that for a moment: It clearly describes that judging is mental, of the mind, and ego based. Being "judgmental" implies that your emotional, subjective thoughts are not to be trusted. But the opposite of course is true: you can only trust your inner essence, your soul, and God. Judgment does not exist in the spiritual world.

Most of you trust that God resides within no matter what name you give to Him. I'm showing you how to reconnect to your authentic self, with your true Source of unlimited potential and to awaken. For most of you it may sound like God and that's exactly what I mean. Your inner Source is God.

I like to keep life simple; I don't like to give God different names. But you can freely choose whatever works for you as long as it works. You have a free will to choose and to do anything you want to do—you're free. I hope you understand and appreciate the freedom given to you. Whatever name you give God, it represents *The Source of Wealth in You*™ that is: (1) your inner wealth—the God given potential you have within; and (2) God the Source.

THE SOURCE OF WEALTH IN YOU™ = YOUR SOUL = GOD

To me, all is energy. God is energy; it's everywhere; I can feel it. To most of you God is of a higher existence, a higher consciousness. Well, don't you think you are too? If you have developed a higher level of awareness you can feel that higher energy within and all around you. Can you now see the connectedness between God and your soul as *The Source of Wealth in You*™?

God is *The Source of Wealth in You*™ because God is within. Your soul is also *The Source of Wealth in You*™. Reconnect your soul to your physical self and you will begin to create miracles outwardly in the material world. Every human being has unlimited power and potential; wealth from within. It only needs to be revealed. It's being revealed to you right now.

A rebirth within you will occur. You will continue on to reveal yourself to the world where you currently reside, the material (physical) world. You'll then have the ability to look into the world beyond—where you will exist as pure energy! The thought of dying will not scare you anymore. Give your best and pass the test while you're here, on Earth, so you can continue on peacefully!

The Time Is Now! You Have the Answer!

Write the first thought that came to mind and share one action step you will take to create the result you want. **DATE:** _____

SECRET 75 | Human beings are like uncut diamonds: no one sees their true value until they're shaped and polished.

CONTEMPLATION: Realizing the power of the human being was a transformation itself for me. When I woke up to this realization, it automatically changed my behavior toward others.

Very few people are raised in an environment where the unlimited human potential is emphasized. Realizing our potential has been left up to us. On the other hand, people seem to not want to realize their potential for many reasons. It may seem like hard work and most believe they don't have the time to devote to the path.

Until I got on the path to transformation it was foreign to me too. I didn't know anything about my wealth of potential. I listened to a lot of self help audiotapes walking the streets of Manhattan with my headset on but I had no idea how powerful I was until I awakened to it. It suddenly exploded and was revealed to me.

There are tons of motivational, human potential and self help authors with books and techniques out there. I'd been interested in that sort of thing for a long time and was absolutely sincere about wanting to help myself. While I listened to many audio programs, but it was hard to keep on with what I heard. I always felt motivated while I was listening—that is, until something else clicked in my mind. Then I would forget and fall back to the old routine in constant need of motivation. This is a clear example of instability and relying on outside Sources for inspiration, survival, and happiness.

For example, I used to live in West Hollywood a few years ago. My neighbor was a lady who'd been studying with a guru for 20 years. She met him when she was only 20 years old. Unfortunately, I seemed to be the only person with whom she was friendly with or could speak with, or even tolerate. She also practices yoga daily. Every time I saw her she looked unhappy but swore by her life teacher-guru of many years.

Don't hand your life over to anyone. You can shape your own destiny. The power is in you to do the shaping and polishing. Seek guidance and connect with a teacher, but understand that no one else can do it for you but you!

The Time Is Now! You Have the Answer!
Write the first thought that came to mind and share one action step you will take to create the result you want.　　🌿Date:_____

Secret 76 | A balanced resolution is always available from within.

Contemplation: Human nature has the tendency to go either all the way to the left or all the way to the right; think of politics or religion. This is called bipolarity.

It is said that a large number of people in our society today suffer from bipolar disorder—roughly two percent—and it happens especially to creative people, like artists. But there's an artist in each one of us, and in my view bipolarity is in everyone. It's labeled as a disease for an excuse to prescribe more medications. One or two medications are good, but the "cocktails"…I need to try it first myself before it's given to you—just kidding.

Human beings are bipolar. It's the type of existence we lead on Earth—a dual existence. Think of going back and forth each day trying to make a decision or to a resolve a problem—you go from one extreme to another looking for answers. You have mood swings because you're a feeling creature. That's fundamentally who we are.

On the other hand, your natural subconscious tendency is to seek a balanced resolution to any problem, to move closer to the middle. I know people who spend their life "thinking" and never seem to resolve much. In that case, I propose that you leave the problem (and the person concerned with it) alone—detach from it. Spend time with your inner Source, your soul by being absolutely alone in complete silence, breathing without thinking, and either the problem you had will work itself out, or tomorrow a resolution will suddenly come to mind. Recognize it when it arrives. There are no foreign terms to learn or a need to get weird about the process of transformation and enlightenment. What I see out there—which makes me laugh—is that people get so caught up in the idea of it and they start acting like they come from India by using special terms and exotic phrases.

Keep it simple—because the truth is simple. Consciously become part of perfection, of the perfect universe, God, by reconnecting with the power of *The Source of Wealth in You*™.

The Time Is Now! You Have the Answer!
Write the first thought that came to mind and share one action step you will take to create the result you want.   DATE:_____

_____
_____
_____
_____

SECRET 77 | You have the power to do anything you want to do.

CONTEMPLATION: When you have accepted what cannot be changed, while becoming certain that you can change the rest, some light will start to appear at the end of the tunnel. When you are certain, you will attract the same frequencies back to you. This is when the impossible will reveal a possibility—your possibility, your truth.

I was at my attorney's office one day and he and I were in total disagreement about an offer he wanted me to accept. He said, "Look, Diana. This is the only possibility. It's as certain as the Law of Gravity." He held his pen up above his desk for a moment and then let it fall. "That's how it is," he said. "Accept it."

I totally agree with the Law of Gravity. It's a fact. However, there are many other possibilities in the universe beyond the physical laws. This is what I explore: What happens in the moment between picking up the pen to let it fall again? A major realization can occur in that moment besides logic. It can be a sign of discovering the gold mine within you—*The Source of Wealth in You*™.

"I believe in the Law of Gravity," I told him, "but it doesn't mean that there aren't other possibilities, or everything always has to go to the same destination." His Law of Gravity comparison was good but not enough for me. Eventually, things worked out exactly as I felt within. I trusted myself; I knew the outcome and the existence of another possibility.

I don't go by the books exclusively. I am into breathing. I go by experiment and connecting to the Source within. Experience it for yourself. When you read these contemplations and write your take on what you have read, trying not to be affected by my contemplations, you'll start to unveil truths about yourself. This is what this book is going to do for you. Take only what works for you and move on!

The Time Is Now! You Have the Answer!
Write the first thought that came to mind and share one
action step you will take to create the result you want.   ✎ DATE: _____

SECRET 78 | Keeping a journal will give you a great sense of release and accomplishment.

CONTEMPLATION: Have you heard about the idea of writing down the three things you're feeling most grateful for each day? It's a wonderful habit. It makes you feel really good when you go back and read the meaningful things you appreciate. It is a simple way to express your gratefulness for life's abundance.

I keep stressing the importance of writing because there's such magic in it. I have noticed that some of the most successful people do it too but secretively. It seems like a miraculous conversation takes place between you and the universe when you exchange thoughts through writing. This is why today, emails are in some way the most fulfilling means of getting in touch with someone and why letter writing used to be the best way to get through to someone.

Additionally, journaling is an emotional release. It can also create real focus in your life; help pinpoint what makes you happy, unhappy, what you want to achieve, and so on. I suggest writing three important things you've achieved each day.

One day, before my awakening, my friend Ron and I were talking on the phone and I started complaining about various things. A lot of people would have taken that as their cue to start empathizing with me and to say, "Yeah, Diana, I know exactly what you're going through." Rob didn't do that. Instead, he asked me to write down, to the smallest detail, exactly what I wanted for myself, and I did. To my astonishment, in a little over two weeks from that day, what I had written down actually showed up in my life, down to the finest detail. It also shows that it was coming from my Source, from my soul. Keep in mind, again, that the techniques, tools, and skills in this book must not be abused. There are certain boundaries, God's boundaries, which you cannot abuse.

In addition to all the other great reasons for writing, someday you might want to show your grandchildren what you've written, just for fun—who knows? All of these reasons are why I structured this book as a reflective book so you can write your thoughts next to mine.

The Time Is Now! You Have the Answer!
Write the first thought that came to mind and share one action step you will take to create the result you want.   ❥Date:_____

Secret 79 | Your life seems to be going nowhere. What can you do?

CONTEMPLATION: Ever wondered what the perfect answer is? Make it happen! Create your life! You've been given a wonderful gift—the gift of freedom to do anything you want with your life.

In India, people follow a life template—the arranged marriage—and they make it work! I have lots of East Indian friends. They're practical and know how to create their life.

One of my friends is a 25 year old man I'll call Raj who lives in Los Angeles. He has surrendered to a traditional lifestyle because he loves his mother who is the strong matriarch of the family. He loves to show me his pictures and every time I've seen pictures of Raj he looks like a different person. Who is he really? I wondered. Recently, he went to India with his mom and a marriage arrangement was made in three weeks. When I saw the pictures from his engagement party I was surprised to see how good he looked in the photos. For the first time he looked like an authentic real being, like himself!

The reason Raj didn't photograph well before is because he didn't feel alive. When he felt good, when he was being himself he photographed well and he looked wonderful. He felt alive because he had created his life and his own happiness. He didn't know his wife to be but they looked happy in the picture; they looked like they were made for each other.

I'm sure they're going to have a great life together because they're committed to creating it for themselves. They've accepted the fact that divorce is not an option. Within themselves they've discovered an ability to like what they might not otherwise like and they practice *acceptance*. I am amazed at the Indian culture in general and the children are amazing too—sane, happy, talented, smart and family-oriented. The people of India know how to make life happen for themselves. The people of the United States of America would do well to emulate most of these great qualities.

The Time Is Now! You Have the Answer!
Write the first thought that came to mind and share one action step you will take to create the result you want.   **DATE:** _____

SECRET 80 | Live each day with focus on your life's purpose.

CONTEMPLATION: Most of life's difficulties arise from not living your life's mission, either from superficial idleness, or from pretending you're busy with other things but ignoring what really matters and is important to you. It's possible that you don't want to commit to yourself or to anything else. You may want life to be easy, but when you want it easy, it will become even more difficult.

The material world is not a place to try to cruise through. It takes some focus and work. When you are living your mission your mind is less able to distract you. You won't have as much time to dwell on unimportant matters. When meditation becomes part of your daily existence you'll notice that many of the so-called problems will take care of themselves.

Discovering or creating your life's purpose is essential. It's like waking up every day—opening your eyes in the morning and thinking about the richness and opportunities available to you. Each day is meaningful. You're not built to have a robotic existence—mechanical, preprogrammed, and without meaning.

For example, people become unhappy when they gain extra weight but they put the extra pounds on because they eat mechanically, without thinking about protecting their bodies, forgetting that the extra fat they put on is hard to carry and strains their hearts.

Having a higher goal you're committed to makes you excited to get out of bed in the morning. Discovering your life's mission depends on your openness and thirst to connect to it. Try to connect with the calmness inside you, the region of peace at your center. A peaceful mind is required for direct contact with the truth that resides in you. The true answers will be revealed when your mind is calm, when you have peace from within. The following explains the core of my teachings.

The Source of Wealth in You™ Teachings Core Belief©

You already have everything. You came on Earth with it. It's within—it's *The Source of Wealth in You*™. Rediscover it and reconnect to it! The rest will naturally fall into its place. There isn't anything to look for outside of yourself. If you do, you will keep coming back to the same place to start all over again. This is the way to happiness.

If you find that hard to do, seek a professional to help you with it. Your life's purpose is within. God created you with a purpose. It's inside you and in front of you. Open your eyes!

The Time Is Now! You Have the Answer!
Write the first thought that came to mind and share one
action step you will take to create the result you want. 🌱Date: _____

_____

_____

_____

_____

Secret 81 | How to discover and create an authentic life mission and purpose.

CONTEMPLATION: The people who truly enjoy their life and live in the moment are the ones who have experienced a life changing event, such as being given a second chance at life. Joseph, one of the people who have looked to me for help, is lucky to be alive today. He often talks about the moment he had a heart attack, was unable to breathe and went through a near death experience. And I myself am another example, just like Joseph. My near death experience was a new beginning for me, a rebirth.

Joseph is a different person today, and so am I. He has devoted his life to others, especially his friends and family. He makes sure that they get regular medical checkups to prevent any potential risks to their health. He also follows a strict routine that includes daily exercise, an early dinner at 6:00 PM, and a life filled with love and compassion. Joseph told me about the transformation he went through and what he learned from surviving a heart attack.

Most people are attached to beautiful objects and possessions such as cars and homes because this is what they know in the material/physical world. However, when you make acquiring these objects your life's mission you will not be happy or fulfilled. Eventually, you will get the car and the house you want but it will bring you a temporary satisfaction. Your life's mission will only make sense when it's based on your soul's yearnings.

In Joseph's case, he learned to devote his life to others—not objects, but souls, just like you. If you feel stuck and unable to discover your life's purpose realize that each passing day is another lost opportunity for joy and happiness. When you awaken to this truth you will wake up to your mission.

If this does not bring you closer to your life's mission and purpose then you must create that mission and purpose. Can you imagine your life's mission? If it feels good when you visualize it, it means you have the support of the universal energy, the support of God. You're on the right track. If you still cannot imagine your mission, seek out a life coach, mentor, or a spiritual teacher to help you with it. Don't be ashamed to seek help; if you are ashamed, your ego is damaging your life again.

I have given you many ways to discover or create your life's mission and purpose. But remember two simple things: (1) choose an intangible mission for your life, not an object; and (2) discover or create your mission right now, today, and do not wait for an unpleasant event to shake you up. If you do not act right now, in this precious moment of clarity, you will be pressed to act later on under unimaginably different or difficult circumstances. Do not wait for a tragedy!

The Time Is Now! You Have the Answer!
Write the first thought that came to mind and share one action step you will take to create the result you want.   **Date:** _____

SECRET 82 | Your actions reflect who you are.

CONTEMPLATION: When you're happy you will act happy and attract happiness and positive people with good energy into your life. When you're out of balance, chaos and frustration will follow you around. Your actions reflect the level of your awareness.

For instance, if you're unhappy with who you are but you blame it on your parents, make a decision today and follow through on it to become a totally different person than who raised you. Then you will be a different person. Practice constant self-awareness. Your mind will try to take you back to what may seem an unpleasant past. Apply some effort until it becomes effortless—your own. Realize that choice alone is not enough; it must be supported by action.

There's no one out there who can tell you what to do with your life. You are responsible for creating and directing it. Live your life by the following inner "code": remain true to yourself, to your authentic self. If it happens that you don't like yourself, then either (1) change the parts of yourself that you dislike; and (2) create who you want to be. All choices you make will be attained easier when they're in alignment with your soul. Become who you want to be. Only when you choose or create the direction of your life and only when that decision has been yours alone will you truly be happy.

Many people spend years in study to get advanced degrees only to find out that they do not enjoy working at what they've spent all those years studying. They later realize that they were either lost at the time or they did something for the sake of doing it or to please their parents. The list can go on and on. Many others spend 40 years punching the clock at jobs they hate only to ask what has become of their life when they retire.

Most humans are a walking dichotomy; they are one person in public and someone totally different in private—they are living without genuine identity. Your actions speak for themselves and let others know who you are. Often you keep swinging between your public and private personas, having no idea of who you really are.

Sometimes others know who you are better than you know yourself. This is why I repeat, there's no such thing as a lie. Depending on their level of awareness, others can read you like an open book, without even meeting you or talking to you. You can do the same for others too.

To attain happiness, balance is needed between your inner and outer selves. Unbalanced extremes are contributors to unhappiness.

The Time Is Now! You Have the Answer!
Write the first thought that came to mind and share one action step you will take to create the result you want. ✒ DATE: _____

_____

_____

_____

_____

SECRET 83 | A daily connection with your inner world is a must. It requires a tool.

CONTEMPLATION: Life on Earth is precious and is a gift given to you. What are you to do with it? How can you find out?

I have a friend, a 28 year old man I'll call Bill, who really wants to find out what he's going to do with his life. He comes from a loving home but no one had ever encouraged him to explore the wide range of opportunities life has to offer. He keeps telling me how he is going to "stick to it," or just "do it," and to "never give up"—the usual platitudes. He's positive about it and he wants to "be somebody," and is sure he'll find what he is supposed to do with his life. In the meantime, he works at odd jobs but he thinks about his life the rest of the time. He says he's a "thinker." But right now he seems to be a lost soul.

When I was in Bill's shoes a few years ago I didn't think I'd be here today. I told Bill that it all sounded really good and exciting but I just couldn't understand what it is that he's planning to stick to. Bill knows how to talk the talk but he has yet to walk the talk.

You cannot discover what you're to do with your life through "thinking" or pure motivation. You already have the answers but you need to reveal them from the inside through a daily practice of THE SOURCE OF WEALTH IN YOU™ MEDITATION©—to reconnect your physical self with your inner world and God.

When you want to sing, you hire a singing coach to teach you how to sing from the diaphragm. When you want to awaken, you need to practice daily meditation and develop a relationship with a spiritual teacher and/or a life coach to help you redesign your life and make sure you stay on track.

Consequently, through regular daily meditation practice (of even 15 minutes a day) you'll find yourself doing what is good for you without even thinking about it. You'll be ahead of life's events and life will become easier, flowing like a river. For instance, you'll suddenly start to notice that what has been on your mind to do you have already done without even thinking about it!

The Time Is Now! You Have the Answer!
Write the first thought that came to mind and share one action step you will take to create the result you want.   DATE:_____

Secret 84 | Courage is contagious and irresistible.

Contemplation: Courage and fear are the two sides of the same coin. Courage is the opposite of fear. Fear is also a great motivator. If you're in danger, fear will keep you on edge and alive. For instance, fear will stop you from entering a lion's den or walking across Fifth Avenue at rush hour with your eyes closed. But for most, fear is an illness. It makes you physically weak too, like taking to your bed and curling up in the fetal position.

In the beginning of our life on Earth we grow up with fear because we're helpless; we rely on our parents or others to raise us. When you become an adult you live with constant fear of what the future may hold. What if you lose your job? What if your husband/wife/partner stops loving you? Or leaves? Or dies? Then you grow old and it becomes difficult to take care of yourself. You are afraid because you're getting closer to death. Society contributes to our fears and discourages us from fully expressing our true selves. There are certain rules and regulations that we might not agree with but feel compelled to follow because everyone else does.

All of these fears are valuable if you can keep them in balance and accept them as part of the game of life. But it is important to recognize that your fears are not real; they were created by your mind. Awaken to this fact so you can truly live your life.

To really live is to embrace the opposite of fear—courage! Remember the Principle of the Opposite Action©—what feels hard for you and what you resist doing is usually good for you, at least within God's boundaries. *Success will come to you when you dare to be who you are, and that takes courage.*

Live your life with courage and life's opportunities will start flowing toward you. There's an old expression, "water seeks its own level." Stay close to and be among like minded people. Power attracts power. Get in touch with your own power—the fearless self—and sustain it. Remain this way. The fears you have about not having enough money or "failing" in the different areas of life will melt away as soon as you realize and accept that your fear is unreal and it's a creation of your mind. Connect with the real power within and bring it out into the material world. The only way to achieve it is through an authentic connection with the endless Source within. This is the power of you, your spirit, and God.

The Time Is Now! You Have the Answer!
Write the first thought that came to mind and share one
action step you will take to create the result you want.   ✎Date:_____

_____

_____

_____

_____

Secret 85 | Everyone has their own truth. What is your truth?

CONTEMPLATION: You're an individual with your own Source, energy, frequency, and vibration. The only truth is your truth that comes from your internal Source, your center. Talking to family, friends, teachers, counselors or therapists is beneficial because it gives you a different perspective. You may learn something new from another person's impression and view of you. Listen to people's advice but do not forget where it originated. It is someone else's outlook that is based on their past and experiences and it may work for them. Some of it may work for you too, but do not rely exclusively on it.

How do you see the events happening in your life right now? Why do you think they are happening? What is your intuition telling you? Forget about other people's ideas about it; put them out of your mind; this is about you. You are the only one who knows the truth and can make decisions for yourself based on your own awareness, vision and understanding of the situation, not anyone else's. In addition, because you have made the decision, there's no one to blame later!

There's so much confusion out there. When you start talking to others about your problems who are not trained professionally on how to listen effectively, the facts will get exaggerated, distorted, and twisted into something else. Becoming aware of your own reality is one of the keys to solving problems. When life gets crazy it's best to not overthink. Take the time to find clarity. Each of us sees things in a unique individual way. For instance, a few times when I was talking with two people I compared notes afterward and found that each one of us had a different version of what had been said in the conversation!

Making decisions is one of the hardest challenges you face daily. It requires awareness, understanding, acceptance, adjustment, taking action, and change. What questions are hanging over you right now waiting for you to make a decision and resolve? I promise, the answers are deep inside of you. They are your answers, your truth. Awaken and they'll come to the surface from within.

The Time Is Now! You Have the Answer!
Write the first thought that came to mind and share one action step you will take to create the result you want.   **Date:** _____

Secret 86 | It's easy to be objective about others but it's hard to truly see ourselves.

Contemplation: What would it feel like looking in the mirror at yourself all day long? Pretty boring, right? It's difficult "to get outside of ourselves" and coexist peacefully with others. There are few things as miserable as being too wrapped up in oneself!

This is one of the reasons we exist with others. We are not meant to exist alone; that's why you're not walking alone on this planet. Others are here with you and me for a reason; we are communal spirits. But please, do not confuse this loving coexistence with codependency.

In the material world I look at every encounter and every person I meet as a two way exchange. It's an opportunity for me to see myself through someone else's eyes, from a different angle, to hear and understand the messages they hold for me. It also creates an opportunity for the other person to see himself/herself from a different angle through my eyes and to awaken to the messages I carry for them as well. Please, understand you're not listening for advice but for the hidden messages. These unspoken messages are from the universe, from God.

It's hard to see for yourself and to get through to the human mind because you're dealing with the ego. The ego prevents people from seeing themselves clearly. You can discover or create effective ways to get through to yourself and others by becoming aware of (1) how the human mind works; (2) how a human being listens; and (3) how a human being reacts.

Once you understand this, you'll see other human beings in a completely different light. You'll actually know how to give them a powerful message so it can work for them too and they won't resist your advice. People don't usually listen to what you tell them, especially when you tell them what to do. They hear it but they go on doing what they have always done.

Listen to others and hear what they have to say and take with you only what feels good to you. Most importantly, striking a fine balance between your own awareness and the messages directed toward you from the universal intelligence (God) through other human beings will help you move toward balance in your own life.

How open are your communication and energy channels? Are you allowing a free flowing energy exchange between you and others? How receptive are you to the information God is sending you through other human beings?

The Time Is Now! You Have the Answer!

Write the first thought that came to mind and share one action step you will take to create the result you want.   **Date:** _____

Secret 87 | Truth is the best choice.

CONTEMPLATION: Trust and truth are important values. We live in a materialistic world where humans are often driven by selfishness, or at least what they think will be most beneficial to them.

In the beginning of any relationship you may bend over backward for the other person. In a business relationship, for example, you may offer your new client or customer a great deal so you can get their business.

A few years ago I hired a handyman/contractor who seemed too good to be true. Jerry was a true professional and I was very happy with his work. But as soon as he knew I was hooked on him the price of his services suddenly changed. I kept my mouth shut, but being human I always held a grudge against him deep inside. It wasn't until he started letting things slip and giving shoddy service that I finally exploded. Obviously, subconsciously I was waiting for that moment to let out what I had been holding in for a long time about his fees changing soon after our first project. This is how relationships become damaged; before that, Jerry and I had a great one. Communication is an issue in any relationship.

Establish clear communication from the beginning and stick with what you agree on—don't change your mind or the rules midway. When you want to make a change, discuss it openly and truthfully. You cannot trick anyone so don't try. Another soul is struggling just as you are. The other person knows what's going on anyway because humans are structured this way. Others are just like you—intuitive, sensitive beings.

The Time Is Now! You Have the Answer!
Write the first thought that came to mind and share one
action step you will take to create the result you want.   **Date:** _____

Secret 88 | The truth always catches up to you no matter how fast you try to run from it.

CONTEMPLATION: It's impossible to run from the truth but people try to do it every day. They try to run from their past fears and insecurities. But they will always catch up with you, I guarantee it! The solution is to stop, take a breath, and quit running. The only way to attain a happy and meaningful life is to face your fears, insecurities, and the past and heal your life's wounds today. Then you can begin to live your life with joy and fulfillment.

Take a careful look at your life. Can you see a familiar thread running through it—the repetition of the same mistakes over and over again? How can you cut that thread? How can you overcome the fears, doubt, anger, and hatred rooted deep within?

Your energy bodies—the energy layers surrounding your physical body—would certainly benefit from a cleanse. Lots of people choose to regularly go on a diet cleanse taking herbs to allow their digestive systems to clear. It works the same way with your energy bodies. Heal your energy and discard the baggage accumulated throughout many lifetimes. Take a look at the issues and resolve them. There's no benefit of carrying them around.

Make a decision this very moment and commit to it. It's better done sooner than later because the more there is to discard the harder it is to do.

Two people who have come to me for guidance recently had their energy bodies in such dire need of healing that I knew there wasn't much I could do for them at the time. Their energy needed to be thoroughly cleansed and balanced.

The latest I heard from one of them, a man in his thirties I'll call Jack, is in pain, needs back surgery, and his cholesterol is sky high. Jack is always running around. I've observed him for some time now. He's always working on a "thousand" different projects and does not have time for himself. He is running away from himself. Jack is afraid to face the fears in his life. He complains about his bad marriage and what a terrible wife he has and how his kids are acting weird. I've tried to awaken him to the fact that what is happening in his life is a reflection of who he is. I offered to take him to an energy healer, but he refused. I even found him another coach; he told her that he wanted to work with her but didn't return any of her phone calls. Jack has some work to do. I hope he can finally realize the mess he's making for himself, his family, his kids, and the world he lives in. I know that he will soon realize that he cannot keep running forever; the problems he's been trying to avoid are finally catching up with him and affecting him, especially his health.

Whatever you're running away from will chase you until you face it. Make a decision today!

The Time Is Now! You Have the Answer!
Write the first thought that came to mind and share one action step you will take to create the result you want.   **Date:** _____

SECRET 89 | Do you want the truth? Light is the truth. Light is unity.

CONTEMPLATION: What is truth? The only truth is your own perception of the truth. There is no such thing as pure truth on planet Earth because of the dual nature of this world.

You constantly search for happiness, for light. Light is happiness. Creating and bringing in more light on Earth is the greatest mission one can have. It would make anyone's life meaningful. Imagine opening your eyes every morning with this thought: How can I bring in light today in my life and in the lives of others?

But how can we do that? How can we do anything to create light in our lives and in the lives of others when we're constantly pulled in the opposite direction all the time?

One of the greatest reasons we came here, on Earth, is to create light in the darkness of pain and suffering. That's even been proven scientifically; studies show that people are happier where there is literally more sun and light around them. In its purest sense, our life represents the struggle to overcome our own barriers and obstacles, to bring us together, to unite the forces that divide and separate us. Begin to create light today—in your life and in the lives of others!

The Time Is Now! You Have the Answer!
Write the first thought that came to mind and share one action step you will take to create the result you want.　　　DATE:_____

DARE TO BE YOU!
SEX IS LOVE!

Do not go where the path may lead,
go instead
where there is no path and leave a trail.

—RALPH WALDO EMERSON

Love is the answer,
but while you are waiting for the answer,
sex raises some pretty good questions.

—WOODY ALLEN

SECRET 90 | You're the most important part of the universe.

CONTEMPLATION: Life is a song, a beautiful song. Learn to sing that song! Sing in tune with the universe! You're an organic part of it and the universe constantly communicates—telling you what is best for you. These revelations are innate.

For instance, when you start feeling that you might be coming down with the flu, your body lets you know it's being attacked by a virus and you don't even have to think about what to do: you feel tired, you lie down, drink hot liquids, get plenty of sleep, take medicine to prevent it, and so on. You took precautions before it even caught you so you don't get sick.

This perfect connection between your body, mind, and soul with the universal intelligence, God, is like singing a song. When you're in tune it sounds good and makes you and everybody who's listening to it feel good. The opposite happens when you sing out of tune—it's jarring, disturbing to the ears and no one wants to listen! When you're in tune with the universe, you naturally know what to do. Each one of you has this perfect connection and can sing this beautiful song called Life.

Share with me, what will you do to bring yourself to harmony—to sing in tune?

The Time Is Now! You Have the Answer!
Write the first thought that came to mind and share one action step you will take to create the result you want.   DATE:_____

SECRET 91 | Do what you want to do, not what you have to do.

CONTEMPLATION: Most people feel trapped into doing what they don't want to do. There are many reasons for this. A lot of them do not own their life or have full control of their ego and mind.

I remember talking with a friend I'll call Paul on an autumn night just a month before the 2008 U.S. presidential election. When I asked Paul whom he was going to vote for he said that he didn't like either of the two candidates but he is going to vote because he has to. That blew my mind. Why would he vote if he didn't approve of either candidate? He said, "Because I've got to." I could see on his face how he felt just saying it. It's very important to vote, but I never understood who was pressuring Paul to go against his will.

This is how the majority of people live their lives. This is the early upbringing family conditioning; the societal programming. This is why people feel inferior, why they suffer from depression and low self esteem. They feel they have to do certain things because their parents, bosses, or people on TV told them "they should."

What do you think about that word "should?" I stay away from it. It's because of the should's, have to's and should have to's that this world is such an unhappy place, with peoples' internal struggles creating more stress and manifesting in any number of physical ailments and diseases.

People are unhappy because they do not feel in control of their lives or free to be themselves. But whose fault is it? Remember, it's always about you. Release the need to blame external factors such as your family or society. You can't change what is, so begin to take charge of your life today.

I live by this motto: "I live my life in a way that's good for me, for others, and society as a whole. I am happy and rich internally and externally, therefore, I am an active contributor."

What is your motto? How do you react or act to the should's, have to's, and should have to's in your life?

The Time Is Now! You Have the Answer!
Write the first thought that came to mind and share one action step you will take to create the result you want. ❧Date:_____

_____

_____

_____

_____

Secret 92 | There is no right or wrong. It's about what works for you.

Contemplation: What is right, and what is wrong? If you follow this model you'll get stuck. You can really open a can of worms if you decide to debate this question. People have been debating it for thousands of years. And honestly, most people still love to talk and talk which brings no tangible result but gives them an illusion of being productive.

On the surface people are often frustrated by being pulled in two different directions. But on a deeper level that is a blessing because we need the two opposites to create light. There are many ways to look at the concept of "right" and "wrong." But I don't want people to get lost in theories. I choose to take a practical approach—the middle—toward balance.

The only correct answer to what's right and what's wrong comes from you—the answer that comes from your truth. As soon as you start listening to anything else besides your own self you might have to see your doctor for some anxiety meds. Seek balance!

Keep in mind the inarguable facts of the material world, such as the fact that an object falls due to gravity. Someone like you and I discovered this theory. Explore another possibility; challenge yourself; revel in the fact that you, if you choose to believe it, are brave and exceptional. It's heavenly when you are simply and purely you.

I, Diana DeMar, came here to contribute to this world by awakening human consciousness and to make it a better place because of my existence. When I say that, I am also aware that I'm setting myself up for lots of disappointments. But it's up to me to let them "get to me." Who can avoid disappointments all the time anyway? I choose to go ahead and to do what I came here to do. I challenge you to do the same—to discover and follow through on what you came here to do.

You are the truth. It's inevitable that sooner or later you will arrive at this conclusion in this lifetime or another. The time is now!

The Time Is Now! You Have the Answer!
Write the first thought that came to mind and share one action step you will take to create the result you want. **Date:**_____

Secret 93 | There's no winning or losing. It depends on how you look at it.

CONTEMPLATION: A friend of mine often calls other people winners or losers. What does that mean? There are so many ways of looking at this concept. But again, if you start looking at all the different angles you'll get lost in a philosophical muddle. Look at the two sides of a situation and balance them out.

Most people, however, only look at their own side. When an issue needs a resolution some don't want to discuss it or are unwilling to talk it over so a middle ground can be reached. Here again the ego comes in to control the situation, a good example of being stubborn or prideful—a common quality among many. This is why we live in a society where chaos dominates our minds and actions.

Unless we realize that we came on Earth to overcome our selfish nature that battles with our spiritual being we're bound to spend our whole life trying to satisfy that selfish nature which will eventually lead us to destruction, suffering, and unhappiness.

So, when it comes to winning and losing, you can think you're the biggest loser or the biggest winner. But the truth is that you win when you surrender to what's really important: your own peace and happiness and a life worth living.

Surrender to authenticity, regardless of the competitive nature of the society you live in. You will attract more and will achieve more balance and create light required for your happiness.

The Time Is Now! You Have the Answer!
Write the first thought that came to mind and share one action step you will take to create the result you want.   **Date:** _____

SECRET 94 | You are an individual, not a follower.

CONTEMPLATION: Individual is a common word and most people consider themselves individuals. I'm curious, however, about the authenticity from which each individual operates.

Becoming the leader of your life and destiny is of the utmost importance. Each one of you is an individual to the extent that you allow yourself to be. When you follow you lose your personal power.

To follow is easy. Most humans and animals do it all the time and love it. Think of how popular Stalin or Hitler used to be at the height of their power. All those followers were just ecstatic. Even in the United States most people like strong leaders or loud talkers who will tell them what to do so they won't have to think or work hard for themselves. People generally follow the way that seems easy and cost free; the way that doesn't require them to work too hard. The same is true in the search for your authentic self and your life's mission. When you follow the path that is easy and cost-free that's exactly what you will get in return: something of little value.

What will make you successful is the Source from which you navigate your life. How do you run your life? Is your ego a leading motivator? How open are you to the outside influences and how affected are you by them? Keep balancing the inner with the outer while remaining true to yourself. This is where the resolution resides. .

The Time Is Now! You Have the Answer!
Write the first thought that came to mind and share one action step you will take to create the result you want. DATE:_____

Secret 95 | A follower is a victim. When you follow you do not own your life.

CONTEMPLATION: It took me a long time to decide on an editor for this book. There were lots of candidates. My problem was that I wasn't "feeling" any one of them. The writings are simple yet profound and timeless.

I wanted someone who could check thoroughly and make sure the content is as simple as possible and easy to absorb and apply. The following is an interesting story of how the secrets in this book reflect your daily lessons and experiences.

When I got a referral for Eric to edit my book, I started to feel doubts about him. It was odd because he had done an amazing editing job on my colleague's sales marketing book.

First, I had to determine why I was feeling this way. From far away Eric's false attempts to cover his expertise on the subject were clear to me. I was also sensing that he was depressed and unhappy. I wondered how he will be able to edit and finalize a life transformation guide—this book? I tried my best to ignore my intuition so I let some time pass as I usually do. A week later, Eric opened up and told me about his background and how active he is in his religious organization. Then I found out that Eric lives by "the Book" exclusively. Like millions of others, Eric dutifully follows the written word of his religion, whether it is the Bible, the Torah or another sacred tome. Yet he is miserable! I told Eric that anything created by humans is guaranteed to have flaws. I also told him that my book is not a philosophy but a representation of the wisdom that resulted from my own awakening, revelations and experiences from meditation. I wrote this book because I want to share it with people to make their lives easier. I want to make life easy, not more complicated than it already is.

Then I shared with Eric a real story about one of my coaching clients who is very successful and famous but also lives by "the Book." I coach this man on a one on one basis. This man is repressed. He's devoted to "the Book."

I'll call him Robert. Robert is really unhappy but pretends to be content. One day when Robert, whom many people rightly look up to and greatly respect, walked into my office and I happened to have some music playing. Suddenly he took off all of his clothes, got completely naked in front of me and started swirling around in circles, dancing like mad.

I was stunned and stood there with my mouth half open, shocked, in awe. At the same time I was happy to see Robert opening up for a few minutes and breaking free of the shackles that were binding his soul. This is what "the Book" did to my sweet friend that I love so much. It repressed him. Robert did not own his life. He became wild when he heard the music playing, trusting me, dancing and swirling, drops of sweat running down on my floor.

Please, read "the Book," the Torah, and anything that is good for you but do not allow yourself to become repressed. Always follow yourself—the ultimate truth. You can still come in and dance naked in front of me! You are a free individual, so enjoy it!

The Time Is Now! You Have the Answer!
Write the first thought that came to mind and share one action step you will take to create the result you want.   **Date:**

Secret 96 | Open yourself to the world.

Contemplation: All of you, I know, are charming individuals blessed with special qualities but there's an energy block that prevents you from expressing your true nature.

The human soul is fragile and can be easily broken. Most people are deeply sensitive and so afraid of being broken into pieces that they cower in their shells forever and don't want to come out. By doing so, you deprive yourself from living a wholesome life. All the goodness inside you needs to come out just as a baby chick has to come out of its shell; it wants to get out and not be locked inside anymore.

Let it out! Whatever got in has to be let out. This is why people are angry, sad, furious, sick, and depressed. It's the accumulation of poisoned energy that turns into a physical illness. How can you take in all life has to offer if you don't let out what needs to go?

Our society is a pained community of repressed beings. This explains so many of the illnesses that plague us. I hope you are not a suppressed being. It's not natural for you to hold on to what needs to come out.

Don't confuse self esteem with ego. Self esteem is of your soul—the real you. The ego is of the mind. In the West self esteem is represented by the ego. This is part of the confusion. How can self esteem be of the mind when it contains the word "self?" This is what the word "self" means: Self—n. the total being of one person; individuality. This is what the word "being" means: Being—n. existence; one that exists.

When you let out what's screaming to be released, you will allow and attract what needs to come back to you. People pay high prices for entertainment because the best actors, musicians, dancers, athletes, public figures, and so on are authentic. People are hugely attracted to that and feel good when they witness true authenticity, aka, "the real thing." You're built the same way; you can attract a good life by letting your real, authentic, pure, and natural self come out.

The Time Is Now! You Have the Answer!
Write the first thought that came to mind and share one action step you will take to create the result you want.   DATE:_____

SECRET 97 | Sex is about creating balance. It's so special—it leads to the creation of a human life.

CONTEMPLATION: Sex is everywhere. A stranger walks by and your heart says, "Yes!" You see a sexy photo in a magazine and you get goose bumps all over your body. You smell a flower or cologne in a department store and it awakens your sexuality, that constant craving inside.

Most people hear the word "sex" and their eyes open wide—partially because sex is such an important part of everybody's life and so many have grown up thinking that it shouldn't be. When I think of sex and talk about it, my eyes open wide too but what I'm talking about is the two opposite energies each one of us possesses within: the masculine (male) and the feminine (female). Sex is about these two opposite energies striving to meet in the middle. This is what's required for balance and happiness.

As we know opposites attract. That's true in sex too as in all of life, energy, physics, and so on. Life is about sex because of this constant attraction between the opposite energies existing in our world of duality. If you are attracted to someone of the same sex, you're drawn to them because of the opposite sexual energy they possess and it's complement to yours.

Is it any wonder why people want to have children? It's because they yearn to express themselves in a more balanced way in the physical world; to create light and life here, on Earth. Through sex, life balances itself out through the opposites (e.g., birth/death, creation/destruction, and so on).

Sex is love. I hope you have sex because you love someone and the calming release through an orgasm is not a priority for you. When you're having sex simply for a physical release you are not expressing love. When you feel that having an orgasm is not really important to you, you can truly love. Again, balance is a must. I'm not asking you to hold yourself back either.

This is why people strive to achieve balance—to bring together the opposites, to find the Technicolor center in the black and white world where your mind (and ego) rules.

We cannot create life without the two energies—male and female. When the cells from the male and female meet in the middle, a perfect balance is created—a human being.

The Time Is Now! You Have the Answer!
Write the first thought that came to mind and share one action step you will take to create the result you want.   **Date:** _____

Secret 98 | Sex is an out-of-body experience.

Contemplation: The family structure in the U.S. is disintegrating if not disastrous. If more people have satisfying sexual lives it would improve our relationships overall which would then strengthen the family structure with love and good energy and fewer people would cheat on their partners.

I have coached men who have been married for twenty plus years admit to me that they would "never" have married their wife if they knew that 20 years later she wouldn't satisfy them sexually. The situation is similar with men in their twenties who come to me for spiritual help. The older men don't get enough sex; they look somewhere else. The younger men are like kids in a candy store; so many sexual possibilities are open to them that they get confused and can't devote or commit to one person.

Men are sexual animals in a way that most women are not. Men are constantly going over the possibilities looking for an opportunity to satisfy one of the strongest of all instincts—the instinct to couple, to procreate. Women must accept this fact and discover new ways to keep their partners satisfied.

This is one of the main reasons marriages don't last: for most men, sex is of the utmost importance, whereas for women it's not—at least not to the extent where it interferes with their thinking or ruins their marriages. The sexual energy release is always good for both sexes but because we're built differently there is a different level of urgency.

This is what sex is:

- Sex is about relinquishing your ego completely while you're with another person.
- Sex is about beauty; through sex you are here to experience the beauty and essence of another being.
- Sex is about creating and maintaining a bond. Sex melds the energies of two people into one.
- Sex is about connecting with another soul on a higher spiritual level.
- Sex is about experiencing God on Earth.

This is what sex is not:

- Sex is not about climaxing.
- Sex is not about competition with one another.
- Sex is not about a physical body relaxation routine practiced nightly to induce sleep.

Unfortunately, in our society few people treat sex as a meaningful experience. Their egos are in total control, even during sex. It's a fact, however, that more men and women want to learn to practice the art of connecting on a soul level through sex. When you truly do connect on a higher level, an out of body kind of experience is possible!

The Time Is Now! You Have the Answer!
Write the first thought that came to mind and share one
action step you will take to create the result you want.   **Date:**

Secret 99 | A real contact with God on Earth occurs through simultaneous orgasm.

Contemplation: I consider the experience of simultaneous orgasm real lovemaking. This is the moment when the ego has surrendered and the two beings are completely connected and in tune with themselves and universal perfection.

True lovemaking is not merely physical; physicality exists only in the bodily connection. It's more than that—it's about the perfect connection that exists through simultaneous orgasm. When you make the process of it occur on a regular basis, the two partners will connect strongly and their relationship will remain strong. It's an intimate communication—a form of talking to each other, a strong bond and an alignment between the two. When you bond with your lover on this level, it is a God on Earth experience.

Sexually most people don't seem to be able to genuinely connect. When two people make love their thoughts intertwine; they melt into each other. You're in this moment to connect with another soul through your body and you want this to last. The process of connecting is the fun part of it. You want to know your beloved, so taking the time for real bonding and joining of the souls is a must.

Remain in this experience as long as possible. Do not end it before your partner. When it feels difficult for you to do so it's a sign to learn a better control of your mind because if you don't, it will also affect other areas of your life. Remember, your mind always gets in the way if awareness and mind control are not practiced daily.

A simultaneous orgasm is a wonderful way to express your respect and love for another person. When there's good mind control in both partners and the two are able to extinguish their minds and egos on cue, the ultimate connection—a God-on-Earth experience—will occur in this very moment and you're in it.

The Time Is Now! You Have the Answer!
Write the first thought that came to mind and share one action step you will take to create the result you want.   DATE:_____

SECRET 100 | Sexual expression and mind control reflect one another.

CONTEMPLATION: Our sexual impulses and desires are connected to and influenced by our mind. As a woman one way to know if a man has good mind control is by the way he expresses himself sexually.

From what I've seen and heard from many women and men, is that most men don't have good mind control. Men definitely need to take some time to learn how to connect their minds to the rhythm of their bodies and ejaculation. It's not easy to do but it would help their lives tremendously.

Women have different issues with sexual expression. They want to let go of emotions, to transcend. Women often suffer from the instability of their moods, which can be a big turnoff to a man.

My female friends, if you're having a problem controlling your moods, see a good doctor or a specialist immediately. Take the time to find a good doctor because you're a priority. If you continue suffering from mood swings and the drama they create, I guarantee you that your man will leave you or cheat on you.

For single women he'll smell your emotional baggage from far away, trust me on that. You think you can fake it? Keep trying and wonder why you're still single. So take care of this today. When women are under the influence of mood swings they look older and unattractive. Your partner will feel less like making love to you—or you may not feel like making love either, if your moods are getting in the way.

You will not be able to look within unless your moods are stabilized. When your moods are an issue (and this goes for men too) you may need to take medication to stabilize them during the beginning stages of your awakening. I know a lot of you don't want to take medication but if it's necessary; be patient with yourself and welcome the equilibrium it brings so you can begin to meditate. Eventually, everything will balance itself out but until you center yourself and learn how to breathe properly, some measures may need to be taken.

The ultimate two way communication is expressed through your bodies while making love. Take the time to learn this type of communication, to experience God and the perfect flow of energy and happiness that will be brought into your life.

The Time Is Now! You Have the Answer!
Write the first thought that came to mind and share one action step you will take to create the result you want.   DATE:_____

SECRET 101 | Happiness resides in oneness, in unity. Sex is unity.

CONTEMPLATION: Let me tell you about a short lived relationship I had with a guy I'll call James. I didn't connect authentically with this man.

Every time James and I got together he talked about how much he cares for the people who are suffering around the world and how worried he is about the war in Iraq, and so on.

Then, when we became intimate we didn't connect authentically. I initiated a suggestion to James on how to connect. What was James's reaction? He turned his back to me by rolling over on his stomach—completely ignoring my suggestion. He asked me to caress his back which I did for five minutes. Then, he rolled back over and made love to me—and, of course, it was for his pleasure exclusively.

The relationship with James underscored three very important points about people in general as follows:

1. ARE YOU "WALKING YOUR TALK"? People think and talk but their actions may be completely different—which clearly describes how one lives an unbalanced and unhappy life. You can see from the example above why James is not in a committed relationship no matter how much he tries to project a loving, caring nature. You can see that he is a man who is confused and has no idea about love.

2. LOVE AND HATE GO HAND IN HAND. It is obvious to me that James does not necessarily respect women that much. By the way, both of his parents died and I feel James had not let them go yet. Most importantly, I'm certain that he is still angry at his mother because she "abandoned" him when she died and he unintentionally transfers that feeling to the women he meets today. Before my transformation, before I began to

meditate, my life was just like James'. But by shedding the baggage from the past and developing my self-awareness I began to understand others; I became more accepting of them and even discovered a way to help them.

3. HAPPINESS IS EXPRESSED IN UNITY. The connection with another person on a soul (spiritual) and intimate (sexual) level is of a higher existence. When you become one with another through sex, in unity, you will feel happier and the other person will too.

How do I feel about James now? I love the human being but we missed the real bond and the genuine connection that is created through sex and intimacy.

Sex, when valued, can do wonders in your relationships and on the journey of transformation and enlightenment. I personally determine the authenticity of an intimate relationship through sex because to me the following is true:

$$SEX = LOVE = ENERGY = GOD$$

Sex is about releasing and receiving love. The way my intimate partner and I connect sexually tells me a lot about the relationship we share.

Most couples suffer from the lack of real bonding through sex. When two people bond and become one through an authentic connection, a simultaneous orgasm is inevitable. We exist in unity. Sex is unity.

The Time Is Now! You Have the Answer!
Write the first thought that came to mind and share one action step you will take to create the result you want.   DATE: _____

SECRET 102 | The child inside of you wants to play. Let it out!

CONTEMPLATION: A couple of weeks ago while I was visiting at a friend's house I noticed that her little six year old daughter Cassie was sitting by herself looking bored and unhappy. When I said, "Hi, Cassie! What's going on?" She replied, "Diana, I hate grown-ups! They never want to play!" She really hit the nail on the head.

Grown-ups forget how to play and are afraid to play. They say they want to stay young yet they don't want to play. Here's what I mean: transformation is a game; it's the only way. Begin to play life as a game to become comfortable with a new situation and to get used to it. Calm your mind so it doesn't play games with you and make you doubt everything. In the meantime, while you're playing and trying to "figure life out," a change occurs without you even realizing it.

Allow yourself to get a little wild and crazy once in a while. Keep discovering new things about yourself. When you're uptight and serious all the time, your energy flow stagnates and you create energy blocks. There's a time and place for everything but fear of being judged by others keeps you stuck and cripples your existence.

There's a fine balance in life. Watch for the extremes you have a tendency to lean toward. I often see people on the path to transformation become weird, way too much into it and into promoting their "BEING ON THE PATH TO ENLIGHTENMENT" in capital letters. Remain simple and natural—this is who you really are. Trying too hard in life destroys the meaning and purpose of living. You're abundance, love, light and energy. Focus on what's already in you!

The Time Is Now! You Have the Answer!
Write the first thought that came to mind and share one
action step you will take to create the result you want.   DATE: _____

Secret 103 | A sure way to remain young forever is to reconnect with your inner child, your soul, and God.

CONTEMPLATION: There are so many ways to preserve the beauty you're blessed with. The following are some of the most important steps to take:

- REDISCOVER AND RECONNECT WITH THE CHILD IN YOU. All of you have a child inside of you but cannot easily express this side of yourself. Allow it to come out naturally.

- MEDITATE REGULARLY. Your spirit is timeless; there is no age or time restriction for the soul. This is why the body-mind-soul connection is so important in keeping yourself young.

- STAY CLOSE TO NATURE AND REDISCOVER YOUR NATURAL BEAUTY. Start listening to yourself. If you take some time to become acquainted with your unique attributes and learn how to accentuate them you will maintain a youthful image while remaining true to yourself.

- BE DARING. Dare to overcome your fears and doubts—the illusions of your mind and ego. This is an essential step to bring out the child in you.

When it comes to youth, beauty, and anti-aging it's all connected to your inner Source of Wealth. An energy block will prevent you from seeing your own reality and making a change in your appearance or attitude.

The secret to staying young is as easy as 1, 2, 3:

- REDISCOVER AND RECONNECT WITH THE REAL YOU! This is not your physical self, your body. It's not a book you study. It's your soul and God within. Then you'll always be connected to the little girl or little boy that already exists inside each one of you. It's there; it never goes away. Need help? Tag along for a day with a friend who has a young child—pay close attention to the thrill of new discoveries and the joy of being that young children possess. Once you reconnect to the child within, half of your anti-aging battle will be won.

- **DISCOVER OR CREATE YOUR LIFE'S PURPOSE AND LIVE BY IT!** It will reconnect you to the child within because it will occupy your mind with something meaningful and will simply give you something to do. This is what kids do—they're "always busy" doing something.
- **BECOME MORE PLAYFUL.** Remain young; don't let yourself age.

There is not just one single thing to do to remain young; it always works in combination as a package. And you know in your heart what works best for you!

The Time Is Now! You Have the Answer!
Write the first thought that came to mind and share one action step you will take to create the result you want.   DATE:_____

SECRET 104 | Your age will become an issue only when it prevents you from making a change and taking a different direction in life.

CONTEMPLATION: Using your age as an excuse or a crutch is common because people are used to the comfort of doing the same thing over and over again.

The older a person gets the harder it is to make changes because of the extra baggage accumulated throughout the years. You start to think "Well, I've always done it this way, so why should I change now?"

Also, our youth oriented society makes you feel inferior, insecure, and even stuck as soon as you reach a certain age. There are many physical acts, after all, that are easier for young people: you're certainly not going to join a pro football team at 60 and you probably would be wise not to try to scale Mount Everest or take up skateboarding at 85. (However, I have seen some people in their 80s pull off some pretty remarkable physical feats!)

Most men and women let themselves go rather early. Take the responsibility; care for yourself to reverse the aging process. Whatever your age, make these changes today:

- REPROGRAM YOUR THINKING AND ATTITUDE. By doing so you will remain young, but it does require a change. At its essence, life is about change—change and action. Everything is in motion; nothing stays still or lasts forever.

- STOP LIVING YOUR LIFE IN REGRET OR SPECULATION. You'll definitely age a lot if you don't stop living your life in the past that's already gone or in speculation about the future.

- CONTROL YOUR FEARS, STRESS, AND WORRIES. Lots of "thinking things over" will leave an imprint on your face; the wrinkles you will get will be like a neon sign telling everybody what a miserable life you have had. There's no point to it. You'll be judged anyway so why not be judged by the number of laugh lines on your face and not worry lines! Now, stop reading for a moment and start laughing!

- LAUGH FOR NO REASON, TEN MINUTES EACH DAY. Witness how free, fun, and playful you become. Tell someone today that you want to practice laughing and you need a partner. Ask him/her to join you and laugh together for ten minutes in person or over the phone.

The Time Is Now! You Have the Answer!

Write the first thought that came to mind and share one action step you will take to create the result you want.   ❥DATE:_____

Our World Is Awakening

The life of the individual has meaning
only insofar as it aids in making the life of
every living thing nobler and more beautiful.

—Albert Einstein

We must never cease from exploration.
And the end of all our exploring will be to arrive
where we began and to know the place for the first time.

—T.S. Eliot

SECRET 105 | Nature reacts as a result of human behavior and consciousness.

CONTEMPLATION: Global warming, flash floods, powerful earthquakes, the daily extinction of rare species…the natural world today appears to be in serious trouble. Have you considered the reasons for such turmoil? I believe some universal energy principles are in effect here.

We are tied to our wondrous planet and it to us. Nature and humans are connected, entwined, and part of the universal energy field, God. We affect the environment with our own energy in the way we treat ourselves and each other—and nature responds in kind. Humans must learn to coexist peacefully with the world around us or we're all headed for doom. Begin today to treat our planet and each other with love and respect.

Always consider the connection we have with the universal energy. Your inner and outer energy depend on each other. For instance, your outer (physical) energy will feel like it's been drained out of you when your inner energy is out of balance. You will not exist in harmony with the universal energy, God as a whole.

Why was there an earthquake in Italy? Why is there a constant war in the Middle East? Who is in control of these events? God? Perhaps. In my view, these particular places are being given a message from God, the universal intelligence, to awaken to the changes needed to take place within people ourselves and to simply get along. We're different on the outside, but we're all the same on the inside. After all, we're all here together connected through energy.

The Time Is Now! You Have the Answer!
Write the first thought that came to mind and share one action step you will take to create the result you want. ✍ DATE:

Secret 106 | Coming up! An emerging culture of freedom, balance, and authenticity!

CONTEMPLATION: You've collected plenty of material possessions but you're still unhappy. You want something else—more genuine and lasting. A new culture is forming right now; it's inevitable.

The people of the United States kept buying what they could not afford to buy—homes, possessions—to fill the void, the emptiness within. This is what led to our current global economic crisis. Today, people are realizing that money and possessions don't bring lasting happiness but only a brief moment of pleasure and it's an artificial and a temporary feeling, like a fix, which wears off quickly. This is what used to make some people keep on buying more things. Like a heroin addict who needs a fix, they're addicted to the brief high that came with anything new and material brings into their lives.

The people of this world are full of greed and lack consideration for their neighbors. Some have forgotten the inevitable connection with each other and with our universe, God. This is exactly what's happening right now. People are turning inward. When your inner world is peaceful you're content and it will automatically reflect out into the material world. The only *permanent* joy comes from your connection to the Source—your own and God. Change the old ways!

When I talk about God, what I mean is God that you feel within and the energy around you, not a restrictive definition from one religion or another. Establish a solid body-mind-soul connection. Nothing will then intimidate or scare you because you will be secure from within. The answers will be revealed to you. It's that simple. At all times you'll rely completely on *The Source of Wealth in You*™ that is:

- ◆ You'll rely on yourself exclusively—for solutions and happiness.
- ◆ You'll spend more time alone.

- You'll connect to the answers and to the truth through your breath.

Our world is awakening. People are reconnecting with their authentic selves. This is what is bound to take place:

- The human being will be able to stand up for himself/herself without the interference of previous conditioning.
- The authentic human being will exist in the present moment—in "the now"—a world more people are starting to inhabit.
- The authentic human being will become aware of the energy fields—of its own and of the universal energy field. Long before the first human existed the cosmos was created from pure energy and now human energy is creating a new culture.
- The authentic being will be reborn and free to love. Priorities will be realigned. You are a priority.

In your life, true awakening is bound to take place when the following occurs:

- You feel you can't take it anymore.
- You have a need to exist on a different level.
- The urge to move on starts to reappear in your life.

I know most of you have suffered enough to get to this point. Get out in the world and create! Do not follow or blend in with the crowd of negative energy! Discover or create your life's purpose! Live it!

We're creating a new culture. It's up to each one of us to make it work. We can do so by:

- Going back to basics: save more, waste less, and control our desires.
- Becoming aware of the mistakes we repeatedly make.
- Striving toward balance between our head and our heart—begin to feel more with our heart.
- Making conscious breathing part of our way of existence.

- Looking into our selves instead of looking for answers in others.
- Healing and balancing our energy centers, our chakras because we're made of energy and we are energy.
- Visualizing our body purified from within and emptied of illness and negative energy we may still hold.
- Becoming love. It happens through meditation.
- Bringing plenty of love into our lives going in both directions—out and in—giving and receiving. Giving always comes first.
- Purifying our thoughts.
- Remaining peaceful regardless of the circumstances.
- Connecting to God authentically and at all times.

The Time Is Now! You Have the Answer!

Write the first thought that came to mind and share one action step you will take to create the result you want.

DATE:_____

SECRET 107 | How are you going to contribute to our changing world?

CONTEMPLATION: It's the best time of our life! The truth is that people are waking up. Most people can now relate to terms like energy, awareness, spirituality, and healing. Spirituality is not just for middle aged or retired people anymore. Teens and young people in their twenties are also soul-searching.

I have friends of all ages. My friends in their teens and twenties are lost and don't know what to do with their lives. They're young and already stressed out! I see them going through a lot of confusion. They pray several times a day, yet they haven't learned how to reconnect to the Source of Wealth within.

Don't segregate yourself from others who appreciate a different religious faith. Focus your energy on the power within—on your ability to create and truly exercise your innate power. I recently met a young man who's a phenomenal energy healer and does priceless work for humanity. It's amazing to see him making such a difference in the world. People are waiting outside of his office hoping to get in. All they have to do is to see him twice a year. How often do you see your shrink? Once a week, I would say, not once in a while. Heal yourself so you can contribute to our changing world!

You're a soul in a human body living in the material world. When you discover and reconnect to your inner Source, there will sometimes be even more struggle and more tension will be created between the two opposites—the inner and the outer. The struggle this time, however, is a sign that you're really living, and it's an opportunity to fulfill a mission, a purpose. Soon you'll be connected to a "different" world. It may seem different to you but the truth is that that is the real, pure you that you just became reacquainted with.

I am not pretending to have it easy all the time but for the majority of time my life is blissful—heaven on Earth! I know it will be the same for you too if not yet because God is within you!

The Time Is Now! You Have the Answer!
Write the first thought that came to mind and share one action step you will take to create the result you want.   ❦Date:_____

SECRET 108 | We live in a world deprived of genuine human touch.

CONTEMPLATION: Touch is a sense but it expresses love. Just like love, touch creates a strong and invisible bond. Have you ever experienced a touch that sent goose bumps all over your body? It activated your energy centers and you felt good, really good. A wave of energy moved throughout your body and the tension was released. It was the other person's energy interacting with your own. When the two energies met it became a soothing experience. A hug or a gentle shoulder pat has a healing effect on people. A handshake enriches the connection between two people. A hug creates an even stronger connection than a handshake.

Of course, many people try to avoid getting too close because they're concerned about hygiene—afraid that they'll catch somebody's cold or pick up some kind of disease. That is a legitimate concern, but how can we have a warmer interaction with others when we don't even feel comfortable giving them a warm hug? Try these experiments:

- Every time you interact with someone see yourself as that person. How would you feel if you were in their body? Think about it. Be conscious of the flow of empathy you feel.

- Look at a person. Imagine yourself giving him or her a warm hug expressing your love. Notice that person's immediate reaction toward you. Even if you don't give an actual hug, I guarantee that if your feeling is authentic you will receive a warm response.

- This one is for dog and animal lovers. To me each person resembles a breed of dog. When you don't like someone, imagine him or her as a breed of dog or other animal you like. Start observing people. Are they like a Spaniel? Pit bull? Weimaraner? Chihuahua? It's a fun way to get closer to people. When you've decided what breed of dog the person most closely resembles, give some love in your mind to that pup… er, person! The great philosopher Immanuel Kant said, "He who is cruel to animals becomes hard also in his dealings with men. We can judge the heart of a man by his treatment of animals."

The point I'm trying to make is simply that every human being can be as sweet as a puppy, a cat, a cockatiel, a pig—any animal you like. Try it! Give an imaginary hug and send him/her your love and let me know what happened by writing below.

The Time Is Now! You Have the Answer!
Write the first thought that came to mind and share one action step you will take to create the result you want. ✒ DATE: _____

_____
_____
_____
_____

SECRET 109 | The inhabitants of our world are robbed of the natural ability to truly love.

CONTEMPLATION: Pure love is simple and easy. But remember, you can't change others except by example.

A few years ago, before my awakening, my life was hard to live because I wasn't able to love. I was empty inside. I was in such need of love, poor me… really desperate for love, living a life of extremes.

The extremes always make us suffer. You've noticed what happens when the weather's too hot or too cold, haven't you? Everybody's sick or lethargic. There were extremes in my case too. I needed love but I was void of it within. I even wrote the songs "I Need" and "Full of Pain" for my second CD *Gypsy Girl*. It took me three years to complete that album. This is how miserable I was feeling inside! Most of the songs, but especially these two, came out of my misery, pain, and emotional turmoil.

Realizing that you're out of love is like hearing a doctor's diagnosis. Once you know the diagnosis, it's often a relatively easy matter to cure. There's always an answer to everything in life.

It took me five years of going through turmoil, unbearable suffering and destruction to find my life's direction. Luckily I was led to it. I was given the gift of a second chance—a second life here, on Earth. By going through these difficult times I found the answers. Through pain you'll find yours. When it really hurts it means you're getting there. That's part of the enigma of life—when you're suffering and in pain it means you're really getting better.

Discovering and creating some balance and becoming love—returning to your original true nature—is what will make your life meaningful. You're lucky because there are proven techniques and tools to help you move toward balance, including the tools, steps, secrets, techniques, and wisdom you're reading about in this book. Begin to consciously apply them until they become second nature to you.

In the beginning of your awakening, try to remain centered most of the time and focus on yourself exclusively. Later, concern yourself with changing the world. By the way, do you realize that you have already begun a conscious transformation toward awakening when you started reading and writing in this book?

The Time Is Now! You Have the Answer!
Write the first thought that came to mind and share one action step you will take to create the result you want.   DATE: _____

_____

_____

_____

_____

Secret 110 | How I became absolutely convinced that people have all the answers within.

CONTEMPLATION: A few years ago I was introduced to a man I'll call Brent. I was inspired and impressed by him. He was the leader of a group and had all the great qualities of a good leader: discipline, integrity and industriousness. Unfortunately, I didn't have time to keep working with his group back then; I had other priorities.

Two years later, I went back to start working on a project with the same group. Brent was still the leader and he and I became close friends. I was shocked to find out that he was completely broke, had no job and was unhappy in his marriage. However, he was extremely aware that he needed help to regain some order in his life so he could create the results he wanted.

Brent had all the good qualities but no tangible results. Subconsciously, he had decided that I would be the one to help him with all he needed. He started inviting me out for coffee or dinner after our group meetings, as friends. He also initiated life coaching sessions with me before I even realized that that was his intention. He was a great example of an individual who knew that he has what it takes to become successful but an energy block that he had imposed on himself prevented him from reaching his goals.

Brent was also clearly aware that he needed the help of a qualified professional to overcome the barriers keeping him away from delivering tangible results and interfering with the manifestation of all of the great qualities he had. He knew there was something standing in his way to success in life.

How did he know that? He just knew it from his soul. During our second meeting I discovered exactly what Brent had been missing most of his life. He needed reassurance: someone to believe in him, to encourage him, to love him, to assist him with his ego awareness and to remind him of the greatness he already has within. He needed someone to reaffirm the existence of his Source of Wealth. He did have a rich Source of Wealth and I knew it the very first time I'd met him, two years before.

I know this about you, as well. I assure you, you have the same Source as Brent and great wealth to draw from. You have the answers, just like Brent.

The Time Is Now! You Have the Answer!
Write the first thought that came to mind and share one
action step you will take to create the result you want.   DATE:_____

_____

_____

_____

_____

SECRET 111 | The answer will reveal itself when you least expect it.

CONTEMPLATION: Remember, the answer is within and right in front of you—always. To live in harmony and reveal the answers, simply begin to practice daily the following three principles:

1. PRINCIPLE OF PLANTING A SEED©

Plant a seed and begin to take care of it—it represents you nurturing your soul. Once you've started to water it, fertilize it, watch it grow and harvest the fruit, then you can help others plant their own seeds, creating a garden of beautiful plants that will bring more beauty into this world to inspire the universe. Keep taking care of the beautiful flower that you are.

2. PRINCIPLE OF GIVING©

Your energy channels are in constant need to release outwardly. This is what's required for a healthy mind-body-soul connection. When you keep holding off the need to release your energy you block the natural energy flow. When you interfere with the exchange of energy through giving you start rotting inside like overripe apples that fell from the tree: never picked, shared, or enjoyed. This is when misery and unhappiness start to appear. Human beings are blessed with freedom of expression. Freedom is about openness in the energy flow without stagnation. Learn to always give first to yourself. Develop your self knowledge so you can give of the "genuine you" to others. Give yourself the gift and practice of meditation. Live your life in this present moment! Take action without expectations of getting back in return! This is how you apply unconditional love through giving.

3. Principle of Letting Go©

You have been asking the questions for a long time and have thought a lot about your life. You may be lost and confused. The universe is perfect; trust this fact. Now, let go of whatever you're struggling with and stop thinking and asking others for the answers. Remove your focus from whatever is troubling you. Detach yourself from it. You have asked and thought enough about it—the subject has been exhausted. Just let it go and move on to something else. Suddenly, when you have allowed the energy flow to readjust on its own and to pass through the obstacles of your mind and thought, the answer will reveal itself to you out of nowhere and you will recognize the authenticity of it. You will feel relieved and you will smile for all the trouble and worries you've put yourself through.

Inherently, nature takes its own course and will definitely involve you because you're part of nature! It is always best to let it happen naturally, whatever that is.

The Time Is Now! You Have the Answer!
Write the first thought that came to mind and share one action step you will take to create the result you want.   Date: _____

SECRET 112 | When you feel your buttons pushed, discover a blessing and a lesson beneath the annoyance.

CONTEMPLATION: On the road to my transformation, I learned that the greatest message I needed to awaken to at the time was often coming from the person who was pushing my buttons—making me feel like a bomb that was about to go off. Why, I began to ask myself, is this person making me feel so out of control? Later I realized that I had an issue to deal with internally that I hadn't resolved yet. There's always something to resolve; remember, you're on a journey called Life and things will keep coming up. But it doesn't have to become a problem. In fact, it's a blessing.

Remember this; it's a valuable lesson and it will save you lots of disappointments. The problem and the resolution are always within where the truth lies. You're the Source so dig into your mine of gold and reject the temptation to blame others for your feelings. Care enough about yourself to take responsibility and to resolve your own issues.

Here's another example from my life. I was working with an attorney on a major business deal. (You may remember the other attorney I mentioned, the one who insisted on his logic over what I knew was true for me—but believe me, I haven't learned all the important lessons from attorneys!) I really needed this person to execute the deal for me but deep inside I just didn't like working with him. First, he sounded like a nagging father. Second, I just wanted the whole thing to be over with; it had been taking way too long and I was burnt out. So I decided that the next time he called I would ask him to stop the phone calls and to start communicating through emails instead. That way, I told myself, I wouldn't hear his nagging voice and blow up at him, jeopardizing the entire business relationship.

The next time he called, I mechanically picked up the phone despite myself. We had a small chat about business. Then somehow out of nowhere, unintentionally, he started talking about something that had nothing to do with our business. It touched on a personal issue that I was ignoring and it taught me an amazing lesson. I was hooked—it rang a bell deep within me. I needed to come to terms with what was damaging my life, career, and relationships and so I did.

That little conversation even helped me clarify some of my writing in this book. The lesson I learned was acceptance. There was obviously a reason why I was getting aggravated each time he called. I didn't want to listen to him, but I did and sure enough he taught me a priceless life lesson.

The Time Is Now! You Have the Answer!
Write the first thought that came to mind and share one action step you will take to create the result you want. 🖋 DATE: _____

_____

_____

_____

_____

SECRET 113 | Your current life is only a moment of the big picture, of eternity. You are forever.

CONTEMPLATION: Have you noticed that as soon as you think you've accomplished a goal there's more you want or feel you need to do? Look at some real life examples. It may be a short time or a few years after you get your Bachelor's degree, for instance, then you move on to get your Master's degree and later you decide to earn your PhD. Or, when you become an MD, completing your schooling and residency is just the beginning of a never ending acquisition of new information; studies and new medicines come out every day that you must learn.

Now, that's just one example. But this same scenario continues to play itself out in some way on some level in every area of our lives, not just academics.

On a spiritual level, you're a soul and a continuation of what you were before you came here on Earth, where you reside in a physical body for a short period of a lifetime. But your spirit continues on.

The concept of time is man made; it exists only in the world we now live in, in the physical world, for the mind to be able to conceptualize past, present, and future. The material world is a messy world so we need order and structure, therefore, a measure: time.

The infinite energy that you are exists through time back to the infinite or back to time again—all depending on the cycle of life you're in. Time has meaning only when you're here, on Earth. The energy that you are, however, is eternal and timeless.

Human desires never end. Why? It's because deep within on a spiritual and subconscious level you know you're part of the big picture; the infinite, endless world where you come from. So you keep searching, yearning to reconnect to it.

You will not end. Realize and accept it so your life will become easier because you will begin to take life less seriously. You have existed before. You're here now. You will eventually transcend to another dimension, in a different form, or you will come back here again in the same form (a physical body) or another form. When you advance in your meditation practice you'll know this for sure.

How does the knowledge and certainty of your eternal existence affect your life today? Have you considered how many times you are going to return to the material world starting all over again, going through the pain and suffering each time you come back here? The choice is yours on a spiritual level. While on Earth we're given an incredible opportunity to break the cycle of repeating the same mistakes and the cycle of birth and death. Now share with me, what exactly will you do to break this pattern and to rise to a different level of existence?

The Time Is Now! You Have the Answer!
Write the first thought that came to mind and share one
action step you will take to create the result you want.   🖋Date:_____

_____

_____

_____

_____

Secret 114 | Cherish, preserve, improve, and don't take for granted all that has been given to you.

Contemplation: I value beauty. Every morning I look at the beautiful home I'm blessed with and the plants that make it alive and lovely and I feel peaceful. To honor that feeling, I keep improving my home—I clean it every day; my plants are happy and green because I water and fertilize them too. These activities add a sense of order to my daily life. There's so much given to you: cherish and appreciate it!

A friend of mine, Matt, used to help me fix things around the house. Every time he started fixing something he would either break something else or make a huge mess. I finally stopped asking him for help; we're not even close friends anymore. According to Matt, things are there to be fixed; "You break it, you fix it."

Without being judgmental, I remember during the eight months we were friends that nothing seemed to be fixed in his life—his car, his job, his relationship with his father, sisters, and so on. I really didn't like Matt's destructive tendencies—carelessly breaking things and then spending so much time to fix them.

Life on Earth can be complicated. Why do we have to make it even more so, especially when our time here in the material (physical) world is limited? Consider the beauty that's around you and do all you can to preserve it and to make it even more beautiful. Have you asked yourself this question: How can I make this world a better place today because of my existence here on Earth? I ask myself and answer this question each day.

Human nature has destructive tendencies. It seems to come naturally to human beings to destroy what's been given to them. Look what we've done to Earth. We came here for a good reason but we've destroyed so much of it. We're paying a high price for it now. Remember, there is always a price to pay.

The best daily life success tool is to practice mind control and self-awareness. Every time you have an impulsive thought it will turn into an impulsive action. Recognize an impulsive thought and refuse to accept it. Catch yourself before you act impulsively and detach yourself. Let it go for a while. When you return to it, it will feel different and you will act in a more balanced way.

This current life is given to you for a reason. Don't take it for granted because it can easily be taken away from you.

The Time Is Now! You Have the Answer!
Write the first thought that came to mind and share one action step you will take to create the result you want.   ♥Date: _____

_____

_____

_____

_____

SECRET 115 | The status quo will take away your soul and happiness.

CONTEMPLATION: The first time I met Dr. Lee, a talented family practice physician, he had just become engaged to his girlfriend of six years. He mentioned that he was not the marrying type but his fiancée wanted to make the relationship "officially forever" by signing the "Marriage Certificate."

I knew that I was dealing with a man who is not living an authentic life; he is going to get married "to please" someone else. I could also see that he would not feel complete if he is not in a relationship, so he stayed in one even if it wasn't ideal for him.

The next time I spoke with Dr. Lee, I found out that he had bought a cockatiel as a Christmas gift for his fiancée. But she wasn't an animal lover and didn't like the bird. He, however, loved the bird and he told me that he could not live without it! Since he had spent most of his life in study and starting his medical practice he now felt a need to take some time for himself so he and his fiancée were not planning to have a child. He added that she is 45 years old and it's too late to have a baby anyway.

What I saw in his love for the cockatiel was a man who had a lot of love within. Beyond that I intuitively felt that Dr. Lee had all the essential qualities to become a great father. That was another warning sign that Dr. Lee was not living an authentic true to his soul life. I also knew that this man is an exceptionally talented physician but has not yet reached the level of success he deserves because he somehow has not been able to live up to his true potential.

The next warning sign was that Dr. Lee is afraid to take risks. His happiness and security depended on someone else—in this case, his fiancée. Then he mentioned that he is "48 years old" in a tone of voice that indicated "it's time for me to grow up." (He had been married once before, but it didn't work out.) The list can go on and on.

Dr. Lee comes from a Chinese background and part of the issue comes from the pressure of being raised in a conservative family structure. One way he rebels against the constrictions of that background is through the private sexual fantasies that he trusted me enough to share. To most of you his fantasies would most likely sound perverted, weird, and even disgusting. I'm grateful, however, that he was able to open up to me. He is not alone, poor Dr. Lee, in having such fantasies. They are a symptom of the caged and inauthentic nature of his life and the lives of many others too.

Dr. Lee has all it takes to become a successful physician and all the great qualities to live an authentic, happy, and fulfilling life. Instead he is living a life of fear and guilt.

I will leave it up to you to draw your own conclusions from this example. I am not here to judge anyone. I am here to give you knowledge through real-life examples and to assist you to awaken to your inner Source of happiness.

The Time Is Now! You Have the Answer!
Write the first thought that came to mind and share one action step you will take to create the result you want.   ❥Date:_____

Secret 116 | How will you know if you're awake?

CONTEMPLATION: While reading and writing in this book you'll start to awaken. What happened to me is going to happen to you too—you will reach into your Source of Wealth. By writing down your thoughts, after each contemplation you'll begin to communicate and connect your own energy with the universal energy. I know there's a lot you really want to share and change about yourself because it's been bothering you.

Four years ago I was quite a mess and thoroughly unhappy. I let the circumstances of my past affect me so badly that I became miserable. But life caught me in time and I made the change required. I know you have gone through a lot. This is why you seek God, peace, joy, happiness, transformation, and enlightenment.

I'd like to share with you something that happens to me on a daily basis. When I sit in front of my computer during my working hours there are times when I feel compelled to leave what I'm doing to go into my sacred place (in my bedroom), the place where I connect with God. This sudden urge in my body and consciousness shows me that I already know what this connection feels like and my soul has developed a thirst for it. It expresses my need to connect with the infinite, with the divine, with God.

Another new feeling that arose out of my awakening is that now I need to have live plants all around me. I have planted flowers and trees and shrubs around my house, both outside and inside and the time I spend taking care of them feels pure and peaceful. I have a busy schedule but connecting with nature now is a necessity for me. Plants produce oxygen and we cannot exist without oxygen—so we cannot exist without plants. Often I bring home a beautiful bouquet of flowers. I keep asking myself, how were these gorgeous flowers created? Who spent the time to paint them with these vibrant colors? The answer is Nature, God, of course.

Now, too, in the middle of a busy day I often find myself just looking at my two little dogs—Wally and Leo—with amazement; at their beauty and the way their faces are shaped, one with his ears pointing up and the other with its ears always hanging down. I ask myself, how did this happen? Who made this choice and a creature so perfect that it looks like a painting?

Before my awakening these questions were unknown to me. I say that my CD *Gypsy Girl* is from "before the transformation" because it represents the true agony I was in back then. But I did not give up; I had hope. Test yourself daily to see how awakened you are. It's fun. Notice what really matters to you now, today.

The Time Is Now! You Have the Answer!

Write the first thought that came to mind and share one
action step you will take to create the result you want.   🌿Date:_____

_____

_____

_____

_____

Secret 117 | The book of wisdom is within; you are the book.

CONTEMPLATION: When you read a book, keep in mind that writing is an expression of oneself. Take from the author's knowledge and ideas only what feels good to you and what works for you. There are many different teachers and books to bring you closer to enlightenment. Where do they all come from? They came from humans. You might want to argue and tell me they were exceptional human beings. Of course they were! But so are you! I am not saying that everyone is Socrates or Goethe but everyone can do what they did—get in touch with the greatness within and *Awaken to the Source of Wealth in You*™.

Do not blindly follow anyone's teachings. You are trained to follow; that is something you learned from the world you live in. Success comes to those who overcome the impulse to follow. Release the need to follow and the desperation for recognition and you will get in touch with your own power.

Lead yourself to your truth! You will become empowered, confident and enlightened. Reconnect with your inner essence and God and you'll become a brand new human being. Awaken and express yourself!

The Time Is Now! You Have the Answer!

Write the first thought that came to mind and share one action step you will take to create the result you want.

Date:

Diana DeMar

*Today, I am certain—I come from beauty.
I exist to create more beauty
and to ultimately return back to beauty.*

Summary of the 117 Secrets

Get Started — 21

Secret 1 | A solid inner foundation is the groundwork for an authentic life. 22

Secret 2 | When the foundation is solid the house can be built. 23

Secret 3 | Discover an incredible opportunity; a possibility in each question you have. 25

Secret 4 | What you truly need will arrive. It depends solely on your readiness for it. 26

Secret 5 | Meditation will take you home to your true nature that is love. 27

The Source of Wealth in You™ Meditation© 28

Secret 6 | Believing in yourself is a sure way to happiness. 29

Secret 7 | All you need is love. Love is energy. 31

Secret 8 | The Principle of Restriction© will bring miracles into your life. 33

Principle of Restriction© 34

Resolve The Past; Remain in the Present — 35

Secret 9 | If your past causes you to suffer today, accept and release it now and forever. 36

I Release My Past Meditation© 37

Secret 10 | Unresolved life issues will turn into physical illness. 38

Secret 11 | How I transformed myself and became the Source of light. 40

Principle of the Opposite Action© 41

Secret 12 | Let go of the past; it's gone anyway. 42

Secret 13 | Become aware of what your soul needs, not what your body wants. 43

Principle of Selective Desire© 44

219

Secret 14 | Addictions will block the perfect energy flow of happiness.... 45

Secret 15 | When you come from a place of need, your life is guaranteed to turn into a mess. 46

Secret 16 | Life is beautiful. Contribute to its beauty through conscious control of your addictions. 48

Secret 17 | The highest form of personal power is to completely surrender your desire to control. 49

Secret 18 | Desperation cripples human existence. Letting go of your desperation will open the energy flow to receive. 51

Secret 19 | When you stop thinking about the future your real life can begin. 53

Secret 20 | The present moment is your only refuge from a painful past or unrealistic expectations about the future. 54

Release The Emotional Mind and Ego Traps   57

Secret 21 | Your mind is powerful. 58

Secret 22 | Your mind is a wanderer. It keeps traveling back through the past or into the future. 59

Secret 23 | Beware of your mind. Its nature is to play tricks on you. 60

The Source of Wealth in You™ Ego Principle© 61

Secret 24 | One single thought can affect your whole day. 63

Secret 25 | Caring for yourself, letting go, and controlling your mind will bring success into your life.. 64

Secret 26 | Your mind says, "No" but your spirit says, "Yes, yes, yes!".... 67

Create Yourself!   69

Secret 27 | I am who I am. But who and what am I?. 70

Secret 28 | How can I find out who I am and why I am here today?...... 70

Secret 29 | This lifetime is an opportunity to become one with yourself and God. 72

Secret 30 | You came on Earth to create your life just as God created you.. 73

Secret 31 | We come from perfection. Our life's purpose is to reconnect with it. 75

Secret 32 | If you want an answer and you're confused about your life, keep searching within. The only true answer can be found in you. 76

Secret 33 | One of the greatest reasons we came here is to discover, to express a unique gift and to use it for the goodness of all. 77

Secret 34 | Just like your fingerprints, your gift is uniquely yours. Expressing it is your life's mission, purpose and way to happiness. 79

Secret 35 | We came into this world to transform our negative nature into positive. 81

Secret 36 | You're exceptional, accept it! 82

Secret 37 | In fact, you're a genius!. 84

Secret 38 | There's always an exception to the rule and you're it! 86

Secret 39 | Aim daily toward balance! Trust yourself! 88

Balancing Act Principle© **88**

Everything Is Energy 91

Secret 40 | There are no coincidences. All has meaning. 92

Secret 41 | The universe sends perfect messages. Can you hear them? . . . 93

Secret 42 | Thoughts and actions have consequences. 95

Secret 43 | The Principle of Cause and Effect© is inescapable. Time may be the only delay.. 96

Secret 44 | You create your life with each thought. 97

Secret 45 | You are life; you are energy. It's about you.. 99

Secret 46 | The human energy field is tied to its surroundings. The perfect connection between the two represents inner peace and happiness. 100

Secret 47 | Your energy mirrors all you encounter.. 101

Secret 48 | Your energy affects the whole universe. 102

Principle of Transferable Energy© **103**

Secret 49 | When a word comes out of your mouth, witness how it becomes a reality. 104

Secret 50 | The universe gives you a message with every encounter and a new lesson to learn. 106

Secret 51 | The beauty of the present moment is in opening up to the possibilities of tomorrow.. 107

Change!   109

Secret 52 | When pain and suffering become unbearable, the human being changes and transforms. 110

Secret 53 | You are afraid today because you don't want to repeat the mistakes you made yesterday. 111

Secret 54 | Your transformation feels easy, free-flowing, and natural. . . . 112

Secret 55 | Control your selfish desires and begin today to practice the Principle of Giving©. 114

    Principle of Giving© 114

Secret 56 | Keep giving without being concerned about receiving. 116

Secret 57 | Transform your desires for your own and the benefit of all. . . 117

Discover the Balance   121

Secret 58 | Life on Earth is only a passing moment, a tiny part of the big picture—of eternity.. 122

Secret 59 | Life is a continuous journey without an ending or destination. You're forever! 123

Secret 60 | Acknowledge what your life is worth to you.. 124

    I Release the Abundance That I Am Affirmation© 125

Secret 61 | Life on Earth is like a dream. You cannot allow yourself to take it too seriously. 126

Secret 62 | What you need is right in front of you. As soon as you wake up you'll recognize it. 127

    Rhythm of Your Heart Awakening Meditation© 128

Secret 63 | What is my soul's mission for this particular lifetime on Earth? 129

    My Soul's Mission Affirmation© 130

Secret 64 | Life is about simplicity. Release the obsession to try so hard in life! 131

Secret 65 | Life is about working smart.. 133

Secret 66 | Life can become a vicious circle. 134

Secret 67 | Life is about beauty—representing and creating it by taking care of your inner and outer self.. 135

Secret 68 | Live your life with pure intentions. 137

SUMMARY OF THE 117 SECRETS | 223

Secret 69 | Producing works of beauty, wonder, and value would make your life meaningful. 138

Secret 70 | Create balance and understanding by looking at the two sides of the same coin. 139

Secret 71 | Spirituality and science coexist in balance. 140

Secret 72 | There is a perfect balance between science and spirituality—a survival tool for the material world.. 142

You're the Source of Wealth 145

Secret 73 | You're the Source of incredible wealth—a mine full of gold. . . 146

Secret 74 | God is The Source of Wealth in You™. 147

Secret 75 | Human beings are like uncut diamonds: no one sees their true value until they're shaped and polished. 149

Secret 76 | A balanced resolution is always available from within.. 150

Secret 77 | You have the power to do anything you want to do. 151

Secret 78 | Keeping a journal will give you a great sense of release and accomplishment. 153

Secret 79 | Your life seems to be going nowhere. What can you do?. . . . 154

Secret 80 | Live each day with focus on your life's purpose.. 155

The Source of Wealth in You™ Teachings Core Belief© 156

Secret 81 | How to discover and create an authentic life mission and purpose.. 157

Secret 82 | Your actions reflect who you are. 159

Secret 83 | A daily connection with your inner world is a must. It requires a tool. 160

Secret 84 | Courage is contagious and irresistible.. 162

Secret 85 | Everyone has their own truth. What is your truth? 163

Secret 86 | It's easy to be objective about others but it's hard to truly see ourselves. 164

Secret 87 | Truth is the best choice. 166

Secret 88 | The truth always catches up to you no matter how fast you try to run from it. 167

Secret 89 | Do you want the truth? Light is the truth. Light is unity. 169

Dare to Be You! Sex Is Love! — 171

Secret 90 | You're the most important part of the universe.. 172

Secret 91 | Do what you want to do, not what you have to do. 173

Secret 92 | There is no right or wrong. It's about what works for you. . . . 174

Secret 93 | There's no winning or losing. It depends on how you look at it. 175

Secret 94 | You are an individual, not a follower. 176

Secret 95 | A follower is a victim. When you follow you do not own your life.. 178

Secret 96 | Open yourself to the world.. 179

Secret 97 | Sex is about creating balance. It's so special—it leads to the creation of a human life.. 181

Secret 98 | Sex is an out-of-body experience.. 182

Secret 99 | A real contact with God on Earth occurs through simultaneous orgasm.. 184

Secret 100 | Sexual expression and mind control reflect one another. . . . 185

Secret 101 | Happiness resides in oneness, in unity. Sex is unity. 187

Secret 102 | The child inside of you wants to play. Let it out! 189

Secret 103 | A sure way to remain young forever is to reconnect with your inner child, your soul, and God. 190

Secret 104 | Your age will become an issue only when it prevents you from making a change and taking a different direction in life. 192

Our World Is Awakening — 195

Secret 105 | Nature reacts as a result of human behavior and consciousness.. 196

Secret 106 | Coming up! An emerging culture of freedom, balance, and authenticity! 197

Secret 107 | How are you going to contribute to our changing world? . . 199

Secret 108 | We live in a world deprived of genuine human touch. 201

Secret 109 | The inhabitants of our world are robbed of the natural ability to truly love.. 202

Secret 110 | How I became absolutely convinced that people have all the answers within.. 204

Secret 111 | The answer will reveal itself when you least expect it. 205

    1. Principle of Planting a Seed© 205

    2. Principle of Giving© 205

    3. Principle of Letting Go© 206

Secret 112 | When you feel your buttons pushed, discover a blessing and a lesson beneath the annoyance. 207

Secret 113 | Your current life is only a moment of the big picture, of eternity. You are forever. 208

Secret 114 | Cherish, preserve, improve, and don't take for granted all that has been given to you. 210

Secret 115 | The status quo will take away your soul and happiness. 211

Secret 116 | How will you know if you're awake?. 213

Secret 117 | The book of wisdom is within; you are the book. 215

Glossary

Aura (aka the human energy field): The human body is surrounded by layers of energy—an energy field that consists of seven layers of energy called energy bodies. This is where most physical illness originates.

Awareness: The human being's ability to distinguish the spiritual Self from other created or imaginary different Selves. Most importantly, it's about the certainty that all other Selves are part of God too. Furthermore, awareness is the acceptance that there isn't separation but connectedness and unity of it all.

Balance: A beautiful, peaceful connection between your inner and outer world; between your soul and your physical (earthly) existence. Living a more-balanced life will bring you peace and happiness.

Balancing Act Principle©: Bring in the two opposites—"the outer" against "the inner"—together by balancing what you're presented with from the world you reside in (that is, what you hear "out there," which is usually negative) against what is true for you (which, when coming from your soul, is positive).

When you consciously bring in the two opposites together toward the middle, balance and happiness will appear. Practice this Principle in any life situation you're presented with.

Chakras: Within the physical body, there are seven major energy centers located along the front and the back of your body. You must keep your seven major chakras in balance. The following describes the human chakra system:

1. **Root Chakra**—Located in front of your body behind your pubic bone.
2. **Spleen Chakra**—Located in front of your body about one inch below your navel.
3. **Solar Plexus Chakra**—Located in the front of your body about one to two inches above your navel.

4. **Heart Chakra**—Located between your two nipples.

5. **Throat Chakra**—Located in your throat area.

6. **Third Eye Chakra**—Located on your forehead, between your eyebrows.

7. **Crown Chakra**—Located on the top of your head.

Conscious Mind: The human ego or personality of each individual; the physical awareness of Self.

Consciousness: (See Awareness.)

Cycle of Birth and Death (aka Reincarnation): Millions of people and several religions believe you live many lifetimes. You can be born as a human, a plant, a tree, an animal, and so on, and keep coming back in any number of forms. There's a reason for your creation in each lifetime. You keep being born and die over and over again until you complete the purpose for your creation. It usually requires a change within (i.e., to become pure love). Once you purify your soul and complete what you are created for then you'll be relieved from this cycle—from pain, turmoil, and suffering. You will remain just as pure energy. Completion of the cycle means total liberation. This is the purpose of going through it all so you can exist as a soul and be forever relieved from the boundaries of the material (physical) world.

Disease: (1) Physical illness is the result of a disruption in the perfect energy flow within your energy bodies and chakras. It starts on the outside of your physical body (in the energy bodies) and it transfers over to the physical body. (2) Since we're made of and surrounded by energy, the missing link of interrupted energy from the energy bodies starts to appear within the body too; it penetrates into the matter—in the tissues and organs of the physical body—and turns into a disease.

Dualistic World (a world of duality; dichotomy): The material (physical) world we live in. Everything, including you, is expressed in dual nature—black/white, good/bad, love/hate, happy/sad, and so on. The resolution I teach is to always strive toward balance, toward the middle and between the two dualities. There's no such thing as perfect balance on Earth but the actual act of aiming toward balance is what makes life meaningful and worth living.

EGO: The American Heritage Dictionary describes the ego as it relates to psychoanalysis as the "division of the psyche that is conscious, most immediately controls thought and behavior, and is most in touch with external reality." In the Western world, the perception of the ego differs from the East. American culture applauds the sense of empowerment the ego provides, and Eastern cultures believe it to be the root of false and superficial happiness. As always, I suggest that you discover the balance between the two: the happy medium.

ENERGY: (1) The fundamental ingredient of all creation. (2) The constant interchange between the inner (spiritual) world with the outer (physical) world.

ENERGY-BASED HEALING METHODS: Can include any of the following: meditation; Reiki; healing touch; acupuncture, color and sound therapy; counseling (short term); hypnotherapy; regression therapy; Rohun; life energy coaching; and spiritual teaching. Get referrals. Also, see *Resources*.

ENERGY BLOCKS: A disconnection, disruption or stagnation of the natural flow of energy. An energy block first occurs in the human energy field (see Aura); then it penetrates toward the physical body in a single spot (within your physical body). An energy block may lead to a serious illness and death. When a person is sick or unhappy or perhaps lives a meaningless, purposeless life—it's a sign of an energy block. See energy based healing methods to release past traumas and accumulated energy blocks through many lifetimes.

ENERGY BODIES: (See Aura.)

ENERGY LEVELS: Healthy energy means a balanced inner and outer energy (spiritually and physically). Highly unbalanced and unhealthy energy may be a sign of manic episodes—very common in our society. Become aware of the difference between the two.

Free Will: You're a free being, free to do whatever you want to do. Your ego interferes and blocks the freedom you came here, on Earth, to express and to enjoy. Learn to control your mind and ego and you'll become truly liberated. Connect to and operate from The Source of Wealth in You™—your authentic self, the wealth of potential within and God—you will be truly free.

God: God is energy—within and universally around us. God is everywhere.

Healer: (1) Person who is in charge of healing another being by using an energy-based healing method and/or a combination of healing techniques. (2) One who works in cooperation with another (a healer) without any resistance, in complete surrender and trust from the person being healed (the subject). (3) One who heals himself/herself on his/her own. (4) One's intention and willingness to release past trauma, to awaken for his/her own sake and for the benefit of society as a whole. (5) One who transforms himself/herself for his/her own benefit and for the benefit of society as a whole.

Higher Self: The part of your psyche that knows and operates from truth; the subconscious mind, God within you.

Human Energy Field (HEF): (1) Essential part of the universal energy field (UEF). (2) The human existence, in both the spiritual and the material world.

Intuition: Each person's heightened sense (to know, to feel, to predict, and so on) developed at varying degrees—some more than others. The level of your intuition depends on the level of your awareness. The best way to increase your intuition is through meditation.

I Release My Past Meditation©: Take an unpleasant incident from your past and see it as though it's a movie clip or something you're watching on TV or YouTube. Choose only one three minute clip. Imagine yourself standing up on a tall building or even up in the sky so you can watch yourself in the scene below from above. It does not matter where you are as long as you can watch yourself as though you're an "actor" playing a particular character in it, not a participant. Repeat the scene of the incident slowly from beginning to end; step-by-step, over-and-over as it happened. Watch yourself in it until you've watched it many times. After awhile you'll find that the situation isn't yours anymore and you can detach from it as easy as you could from something you saw on TV.

I RELEASE THE ABUNDANCE THAT I AM AFFIRMATION©
Repeat the following affirmation to yourself and practice it daily through your actions:

> "There is a reason for everything. My life has meaning and purpose. I now simply give of myself. I'm discovering new ways to give all the time. This is now the way of my existence. I give good energy to others. I now accept others the way they are because they're like me—human. I give without being concerned about receiving. I am a giver. It's such a release!"

KARMA: What you think, say and do returns to you in the exact same way, sooner or later. You cannot run away from it; it always catches up to you. (See "Principle of Cause and Effect©")

LIGHT: Something that makes things visible or affords illumination. Spiritually, in my teachings, it means creating and spreading love, joy, and happiness.

MATERIAL: Of matter; physical; tangible; of substance; touchable.

MIND: The intellect, knowledge, thought, consciousness, and judgment all humans possess. The mind and its various parts (i.e., id, ego, and superego) and your emotional impulses tend to run the material (physical) world. The world of God and the Spirit is free of the mind and ego. I teach striving always toward balance, toward the middle, connecting the two worlds (material and spiritual). Take the best of the two worlds and make it work for you and for society as a whole.

MY SOUL'S MISSION AFFIRMATION©: Repeat this affirmation with certainty in the morning, as soon as you wake up; and at night, right before you fall asleep. This affirmation works well with The Source of Wealth in You™ Meditation© first. Practice it for five minutes, then repeat the following:

"I am energy! I am a soul residing and manifesting itself through my physical body where I exist temporarily. My body is guaranteed to die. My soul will continue to live, to swim in the sea of universal energy, to embrace, and to interact with other souls in the unending dance of life. But I must complete what I came here to do! I came here to fulfill a purpose. I am now being awakened to my life's purpose. I am living my mission on Earth so I can be forever released from human bondage—from the cycle of birth and death, pain and suffering."

PRINCIPLE OF ATTRACTION© ("**THE MIRROR EFFECT**"): You encounter exactly what you represent at this moment: your thoughts, words, actions, state of being and the people and events in your life. You are energy; you're surrounded by energy. Information travels through energy. God is within. God is the energy around you. God is the truth. If you want to attract something different you'll find it necessary to change something within yourself. That will attract exactly what you've changed in yourself. For instance, if you're now more loving and you operate from a place of love, this is exactly who and what you will encounter now in your life—pure, authentic love.

PRINCIPLE OF CAUSE AND EFFECT© (**AKA KARMA**): Become aware of each thought that passes through your mind. It leads to action. Your feelings and actions mirror reactions. What you do today is exactly what you will encounter—today or at a later time. This principle always catches up to you. Similar to The Golden Rule, "Do unto others what you would have them do unto you," and the old adage, "What goes around comes around."

PRINCIPLE OF GIVING©: When you interfere with the natural release and exchange of energy through giving you start rotting inside like overripe apples that fell from the tree: never picked, shared or enjoyed. This is when misery and unhappiness start to appear. Human beings are blessed with freedom of expression. Freedom is about openness in the energy flow of exchange through giving. Your energy channels are in need of free-flowing energy. This is what's required for a healthy body, mind and soul connection. When you hold off the natural need for release through giving you block the energy. Learn to always first give to yourself. Develop your self knowledge to be able to give of the "genuine you" to others. Give yourself the gift and practice of meditation. Live your life in this present moment! Take action! This is how you apply unconditional love through giving.

PRINCIPLE OF LETTING GO©: You have been asking the questions for a long time and have thought a lot about your life. You may be lost and confused. The universe is perfect; trust this fact. Now, let go of whatever you're struggling with and stop thinking and asking others for the answers. Remove your focus from whatever is troubling you. Detach yourself from it. You have asked and thought enough about it—the subject has been exhausted. Just let it go and move on to something else. Suddenly, when you have allowed the energy flow to readjust on its own and to pass through the obstacles of your mind and thought the answer will reveal itself to you out of nowhere and you will recognize the authenticity of it. You will feel relieved and you will smile for all the trouble and worries you've put yourself through.

PRINCIPLE OF PLANTING A SEED©: Plant a seed and begin to take care of it—it represents you nurturing your soul. Once you've started to water it, fertilize it, watch it grow and harvest the fruit then you can help others plant their own seeds, creating a garden of beautiful plants that will bring more beauty into this world to inspire the universe. Keep taking care of the beautiful flower that you are.

PRINCIPLE OF RESTRICTION©: The mind, the ego, has a tendency to mislead you, to overreact. It's possible that you may react and act in a way that can cause irreparable damage. Take control of your mind, restrict your reactions and remain calm and peaceful at all times.

PRINCIPLE OF SELECTIVE DESIRE©: Life is a series of choices; anything you do or don't do is your choice. Your happiness depends on the choices you make! You can easily select which of your desires to pursue because you're free to do so. You're a human being graciously imbued with free will. To become a contributor and to change the world get in touch with the real you and carefully select and make choices—what to let in, what to keep out and what you know and feel is best for you. Beware of your mind and your ego's desires! Who is running you? You are the only one who has the power to take charge of your life.

Principle of the Opposite Action©: Anything that feels hard for you and what you resist is usually good for you. To execute this principle, remember, do what you don't feel like doing, within God's boundaries. Enjoy the results from a daily conscious application of this principle!

Principle of Transferable Energy©: The thoughts someone has for you will reach you from far away. It will affect your whole being just as if they had physically touched you or spoken to you. Now, remember, you can actually get sick from negative thoughts—yours and others'. Their thoughts and energy will transfer onto you and it will affect you. The same works the opposite way—your energy, thoughts, feelings and so on affects others. They will begin to act, behave, and react in a certain way based on the kind of energy they've received from you.

Reincarnation: (See Cycle of Birth and Death.)

Rhythm of Your Heart Awakening Meditation©: Lie down on your left side. Extend the left arm and place your head on it instead of a pillow and adjust it until you feel comfortable. You will be able to hear your heartbeat very well. Breathe and listen to your heartbeat for ten minutes. If this position feels uncomfortable to you, use a large size clock. Lie down on your back. Breathe consciously while listening to the arms of the moving clock sound. Notice each second/sound it makes. Keep listening for ten minutes. Simple! Awaken to what's in front of you and recognize it so you can develop important insight. By becoming aware of your own heartbeat you'll start to notice some of the other details of life.

Seven Areas of Your Life: These are career; money; health/beauty/fitness; friends/family/relationships; personal development; fun and recreation; and physical environment. (See Wheel of Life.)

Spiritual: Of God; Godly; pure; religious.

Soul: Your essential nature—a force, energy, spirit, the real you and the essence of the physical being. The soul is pure energy. It lives forever.

Subconscious Mind: This is where the truth, your soul, and the history of your soul's journey through many lifetimes reside with God. You already have the answers within you and they are in the subconscious mind. It's a step below your physical awareness (i.e., conscious mind).

THE SOURCE: God; See *The Source of Wealth in You*™.

THE SOURCE OF WEALTH IN YOU™**:** The never ending Source within that is the Source of fun, joy, happiness, love, God, beauty, material wealth, the greatness of you, your authentic self, your unlimited wealth of potential, and so on. Your awareness and connection to it is the answer to it all. Your fulfillment in the material world depends on your connection with *The Source of Wealth in You*™.

THE SOURCE OF WEALTH IN YOU™ **EGO PRINCIPLE**©**:**

- Consciously operate from *The Source of Wealth in You*™ (your soul and God residing within).
- Practice constant awareness and control of your mind, ego, thoughts, actions, and reactions.
- Become practical.
- Take the best of both worlds (e.g., East/West; inner/outer) and only what works for you.
- Release what's useless to you. Take action!
- Always aim toward the middle, toward balance.

THE SOURCE OF WEALTH IN YOU™ **MEDITATION**©**:** The Source of Wealth in You™ Meditation© is a life transformation tool to assist you to return to your real, spiritual, and purely natural way of existence—happiness. It is a combination of different ancient Eastern meditation and yogi techniques simplified into one core technique. The Source of Wealth in You™ Meditation© is a state of being without concentration, thoughts, effort, or focusing of the mind. It consists of conscious and proper breathing. You will become aware of the present moment and will connect to your Higher Self, the universal intelligence, God as a way of life. Simply begin to breathe from your diaphragm while witnessing both—the stream of air going in and out of your nostrils simultaneously with the inhale/exhale of your diaphragm (expanding out with the inhale and going back in with the exhale). Always breathe through your nose and give a nice long exhale. When it becomes second nature to you, you can consciously exist through this technique. Until then, choose the setting and position that personally suits you best. The Source of Wealth in You™ Meditation© is an effective method to be practiced by people of all ages, cultures, and religions because it already exists in you (your breath). It's simple, natural, and easy.

THE SOURCE OF WEALTH IN YOU™ TEACHINGS CORE BELIEF©: You already have everything. You came on Earth with it. It's within—it's The Source of Wealth in You™. Rediscover it and reconnect to it! The rest will naturally fall into its place. There isn't anything to look for outside of yourself. If you do, you will keep coming back to the same place to start all over again. This is the way to happiness.

TRUTH: Your soul/spirit; your Higher Self (aka the subconscious mind); God. What you know in your heart to be authentically true. When you operate from *The Source of Wealth in You*™ and God—from truth, you will feel a sense of peace, love, certainty, fearlessness, bliss, and happiness.

UNIVERSAL ENERGY FIELD (UEF): (1) Energy makes life possible. (2) Energy is within and all around you. (3) The energy all creation is made of. (4) God.

WALKING YOUR TALK: You do what you say you're going to do; your words are followed by the same actions.

WHEEL OF LIFE: It looks like a circle in the shape of a pie. At the hub in the center is you. The rest is cut into pieces that contain each one of the Seven Areas of Your Life. Using a scale from 1 to 10, starting at level 1 close to the center, moving up to level 10 which is the periphery of the wheel, mark the level you feel you're at for each area of your life. When you connect the marks, you can visually see the balance or the imbalance of the Wheel, meaning your life.

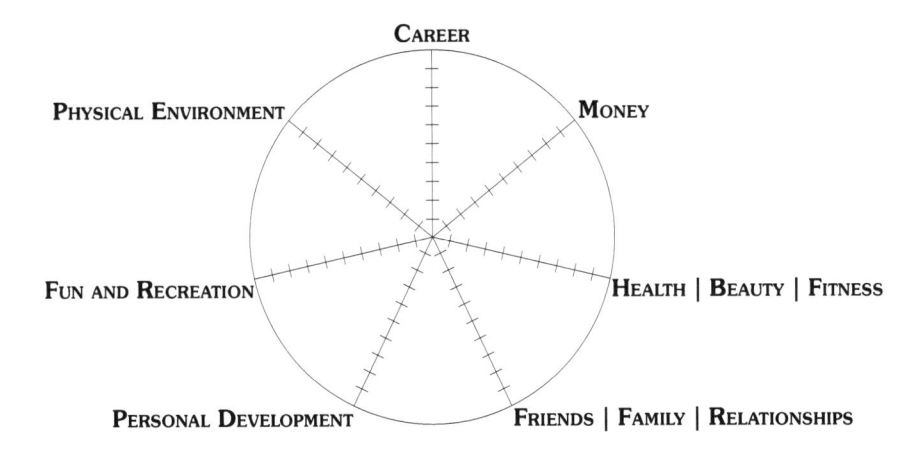

```
                    CAREER
PHYSICAL ENVIRONMENT        MONEY


FUN AND RECREATION          HEALTH | BEAUTY | FITNESS


   PERSONAL DEVELOPMENT   FRIENDS | FAMILY | RELATIONSHIPS
```

WHEEL OF LIFE

YOUR ENERGY: (1) A spiritual representation of who you are. Other creatures, humans and beings are naturally tuned in to your energy and can feel it from far away or in person. (2) The purity, the message you project from your soul and God within.

YOUR PHYSICAL SELF: The visible self, the physical body. It exists in the material world; it is temporary and guaranteed to end—to die at any moment.

YOUR SPIRITUAL SELF: The invisible Self, your Spirit; the eternal soul; your everlasting spiritual energy that transcends your physical body.

YOUR TWO SELVES (YOUR DUAL SELF): Your spiritual self and your physical self.

Resources

I highly recommend the following colleagues and resources:

Erik Cetrulo
Spiritual Counseling, Vibrational Healing, Chakra Balancing, Tantric Healing, Herbs, Energetic Dowsing, and Nutritional Counseling
17000 Ventura Blvd., Suite 220, Encino, CA 91316
Phone: 818-788-1214 | Cell: 559-709-1704
Email: erik.cetrulo@yahoo.com

Dr. Cathryn Hu, PhD
Founder: Advanced Acupuncture, Inc.
1260 Fifteenth St., Suite 60, Santa Monica, CA 90404
Phone: 310-458-2848 | Fax: 310-458-2899
Website: advancedacupuncture.com
Email: advanced_acupuncture@yahoo.com

There's more pain and disruption in the world now than ever. In our changing world a daily application of tangible survival tools is a must. Today, the world needs a stronger authentic connection with God —in each moment, in each breath you take— to return to love and to reconnect to true success and happiness.

DIANA DEMAR

About the Author

DIANA DEMAR, CEC, is an author, speaker and inspirational teacher in the field of self-development. Her writings, life-wisdom tools and meditation-healing techniques are improving lives around the world. Ms. DeMar is a Certified Life Coach and the originator of *The Source of Wealth in You*™ book series. *Awaken to the Source of Wealth in You*™*: 117 Secrets to Reconnect to Your Divine Power* is her first book.

Ms. DeMar began her quest for knowledge at an early age. Humble beginnings and a childhood filled with instability attribute to her strength today. After graduating as a Physician's Assistant Ms. DeMar embarked on an inner journey of exploration that led her to become an actress and singer-songwriter (with several films and CDs to her name). But this was just the beginning. After spending several years in meditation she awakened to a powerful wealth of knowledge, wisdom, awareness, bliss and transformation. Ms. DeMar discovered the endless Source of Wealth within and her writings are the record of her awakening.

The works of Ms. DeMar express the inner essence of the human being as the Source of Wealth and its connection with the universal energy, God. She writes about controversial topics such as the power of the human being, sex, money, religion and politics while promoting peaceful ways of finding common ground through balance, acceptance and authenticity. Her teaching, healing and coaching methods equip people with life-wisdom tools, skills and techniques to connect in unity and to live successful and Godly lives filled with love, fun, joy and happiness.

Made in the USA
Charleston, SC
26 September 2010